Manger and Mystery

An Advent Adventure

Marilyn Brown Oden

UPPER
ROOM BOOKS
NASHVILLE

Cover illustration: © Natalie Jaynes
Cover design: Jim McAnally
First printing: 1999

LIBRARY OF CONGRESS CATALOGING-IN-PUBLICATION

Oden, Marilyn Brown.
    Manger and mystery: an Advent adventure / by Marilyn Brown Oden
        p.   cm.
    Includes bibliographical references.
    ISBN 0-8358-0861-0
    1. Advent I. Title.
BV40.0334   1999   98-55298
263'.912—dc21   CIP

Printed in the United States of America

To my grandchildren

Chelsea

Sarah

Nathan

Graham

who taught me, once again, how to play

Contents

Bringing Down the Powerful
Lifting Up the Lowly
Filling the Hungry
Sending the Rich

Going to Bethlehem
Glimpsing the Star
Giving and Thanksgiving

The Manger
The Mystery

Guide for Individuals
Guide for Groups

Acknowledgments

I WANT TO EXPRESS appreciation for several people who have been especially helpful in my own faith journey and in this writing.

My family, who continue to enrich and bless my life in uncountable ways.

Dr. Paul Escamilla, a pastor who models humility and commitment, and whose writings and recommended readings were a helpful resource for this book.

My covenant group of bishops' spouses, male and female individuals from around the globe, united in faith.

JoAnn Miller and Rita Collett, editors who encourage and support my writing journey.

Old friends who give my life depth and meaning: Gwen White, my mentor as a bishop's spouse and soul-sister in Christ; Gwen Branton, Estelle Chapel, Joanne Greening, Martha Hardt, Bettye Haynes, Carol Robertson, Gloria Slack, and Virginia Taylor, whom I see weekly for study, caring, and sharing; Twila Stowe Bryan, Julia Wilke, and George Baskin, who encourage me on my writing journey; Dan and Barbara Batchelor, Franklin and Judy Forney, Bill and Phyllis Henry, Dick and

Lavonn McKnight, Doug and Mary McPherson, David and Paula Severe, and MacKenzie and Edith Thompson, whose deep and life-giving friendships are rooted in the past and flourish in the present; Stone and Eleanor Caraway, whose many kindnesses could never be repaid; Marilyn Ogilvie and Donna Pendarvis, who have walked with me for many years and continue to share the journey.

Introduction

THE PURPOSE of *Manger and Mystery* is to help us once again prepare ourselves for the birth of the Christ child in the world and in our own hearts. Our Advent adventure will include a special time devoted to scripture, readings, reflection, and prayer—all aimed toward awakening ourselves to the meaning of that birth and, thereby, to living our own lives more fully.

Advent is a time of longing for life to be different, a time of waiting in hopeful anticipation. The word *Advent* comes from *adventus*, which means "coming" or "arrival." The season originated in the Western church in fifth-century Gaul (now France, Belgium, and the western part of Germany). It began as a six-week period of preparation for the festival of the Nativity. Often called "Winter Lent," it was a penitential time with fasting three days a week. In the seventh and eighth centuries in Spain and parts of Italy including Rome, the Advent season started the fifth Sunday before Christmas, and it completed the Christian year (which traditionally began with the Christmas Vigil). Eventually today's practice evolved in which the Christian year begins with Advent, starting the fourth Sunday before Christmas, and ends Christmas Eve. It is a season of preparing for the birth of Christ—the fulfillment of promise, the personification of Good News, and the presence of God in our midst.

The first four chapters of this book correspond with the four weeks of Advent. Each begins with an introduction and closes with a guide for thought and reflection. Chapters 1–3 have seven sections, each with a scripture reading. Because the fourth week of Advent varies in length from year to year, chapter 4 has three sections. The last chapter focuses on Christmas Eve and Christmas Day. The chapters' flexibility offers a choice between weekly reading in one sitting or daily reading by section.

An Adventurer may choose to venture forth alone or to study this book in a special group formed for Advent or perhaps in a church school class that uses this material for Advent. At the end of the book, you will find guides for these different kinds of adventures. It is suggested that large church school classes form discussion subgroups of eight to ten members. That same size also is recommended for special Advent groups.

As Adventurers we will seek to recover the simplicity of the stable, rekindle the sacredness of the Advent season, remember the Song of Mary, reclaim and follow the star, and recall our story and restore our call—our call to live our lives in awareness of God's presence and in responsiveness to God's love. Our Advent adventure invites us to unwrap the gift of full life, boldly receiving it and boldly giving it away.

ahead chapter

Recovering the Stable

ADVENT IS HERE! The baby is coming! The one who can bring meaning to our lives and teach us how to live fully! Let's loosen our shackles and leap into this adventure!

The dictionary defines the word *adventure* as "a bold undertaking, in which hazards are to be encountered," "a remarkable occurrence in one's personal history," "a stirring experience." An Advent adventure is a risky and bold undertaking and, at the same time, a remarkable and stirring experience. It invites us to be awake, to expose ourselves to uncertainty about our destination. To welcome the surprises that unfold, to hear the old story in new ways, to look at traditional symbols through open eyes and hearts. To journey deeply through the season, wrapping our timeworn customs in new expectations.

❖

Arriving home late in the afternoon on this first Sunday of Advent, I reach up high on the closet shelf and pull down a special box that contains our old crèche from Bethlehem. Alone, I turn on Christmas carols and set spiced apple cider on the stove. The aroma of cinnamon floats through the house. As I begin to unwrap the figures hand-carved from olive wood, I can almost feel the touch of our four children's small hands helping me set the crèche up, hands now grown to full size.

Setting up the manger scene reminds me that the layers of Christmas tradition mix together the accounts of Luke and Matthew (the only Gospels that tell about Jesus' birth). More important, it takes me back in time to the essentials of the story, to the sacred silence and simplicity of that night and that place.

I unwrap the stable first, which on that night long ago was likely to have been a cave used to shelter the animals. Next comes the manger where Luke tells us Jesus lay, probably a trough carved of stone where the animals fed, softened with hay that night. Mary's song of praise shines in her eyes as she and Joseph look on, adoring. Two sheep and a cow lying beside the manger represent the curious animals of that cherished night. Young shepherds stand in awe, staffs in hand. Last comes Matthew's magi from the East. He gives no number, but the tradition is three; and they kneel before the babe to present their gifts. And somewhere above is the light of the star, offering direction.

The crèche takes us around the globe into Bethlehem and back in time some 2,000 years. People from all walks of life and theological positions have considered this scene from every point of view. Stained-glass windows, mosaics, and paintings have portrayed it in all colors. Sermons have arrayed it with a myriad of perceptions. What is left to say?

For me, one aspect of Advent and Christmas is necessary yet problematic: The story is seen and interpreted through a post-crucifixion, post-Easter perspective. The early church celebrated Advent as a penitential time, referring to it as "Winter Lent." Contemporary theologians also see Advent in partnership with Lent. We know that Christmas morning culminates in crucifixion mourning, for the manger leads to the cross. Judas casts a shadow over our joy, and the pounding of nails echoes beyond the Nativity. We know all that, but they did not know it—not this small group gathered around the baby Jesus.

What dreams Mary and Joseph hold for this babe! Their expectations began even before his birth (just like those of today's parents-to-be). All babies are special, but this is *the* baby. Mary believes the angel's message that he "will be called the Son of the Most High, and the Lord

God will give to him the throne of his ancestor David" (Luke 1:32). The child in Elizabeth's womb leaps for joy at the visit of the "mother of my Lord" (Luke 1:43). Zechariah prophesies about God's raising up this "mighty savior" to save them from their "enemies and from the hand of all who hate" them (Luke 1:69, 71). The magi seek "the child who has been born king of the Jews" (Matt. 2:2). The shepherds go to Bethlehem to see the newborn announced as the "Savior, who is the Messiah, the Lord" (Luke 2:11). The babe comes wrapped in the expectations of ascending the throne of David; of being Lord; of saving the people from their enemies; of being king of the Jews, the Messiah or deliverer.

And there is also Joseph's dream. He is "to name him Jesus, for he will save his people from their sins" (Matt. 1:21). Perhaps only Joseph foresees that the deliverance to be brought by Jesus is not from earthly troubles and political exploitation but from sin, from greed and apathy and pride. Perhaps Joseph's expectation for the babe is that he will heal the hearts of the people.

But none of these folk, not a single one among them, couches the dream for the babe in the destiny of the cross. As we begin our Advent adventure—just this once—let's stand beside them and leave the cross to Lent and our wandering in the wilderness to springtime. That is part of the story in the fullness of time but not of their story in the moment. Not yet. For now, let's share their focus and prepare for this special birth with anticipation and amazement, wonder and rejoicing. Advent is here! The baby is coming!

Secular Hype and Holy Silence
Scripture: Isaiah 63:16-19; 64:1-8

My husband Bill and I rose in the wee hours of the morning on this first Sunday of Advent. He needed to be back in Dallas by late afternoon, and it would be a long drive home. Stars dotted the dark dome above us, and the sky changed ever so slowly from night to day. Rosy stretches of chiffon brought beauty to dawn, gradually fading to white with the full rise of the sun. Jet planes drew streamers that arched across the blue sky and widened into feathery streaks of clouds. In silent splendor the heavens proclaimed once again that the baby is coming!

God did not send us a global guru or a pompous prelate. God sent us a baby. In *The Drama of Christmas*, Morton Kelsey suggests, "The Divine wanted to attract us, not overpower us."[1] Perhaps God also wanted us to see that the dynamics of preparing and caring for a baby —especially this baby—teach us about the Christian faith. Preparing to welcome the baby with Mary and Joseph and serving as part of their extended family call us to new ways of living and loving.

While driving home, Bill and I passed through a small town at eleven o'clock and stopped at a little church. Barely on time, we slipped into the back pew, wearing our travel clothes and pretending to be invisible. We'd never been there before and probably never will be again. But we knew the customs: lighting the first candle of the Advent wreath, welcoming a new baby with a rose on the altar, and placing the bouquet of flowers nearby to honor the member who'd died that week. We sang the seasonal hymns, listened to the anthem by the choir of five, prayed the Lord's Prayer, and shared a portion of our abundance. The pastor read from Isaiah and preached the Word. On this first day of the Christian year, we worshiped God amidst strangers, yet strangers who are kin as children of God.

The celebration of Advent doesn't change from place to place or from year to year: hanging the greens and displaying manger scenes, ringing bells and singing carols, lighting the candles and reading the story. All around the world on this day, Christians speak the language of love and follow the Advent customs that have evolved over time. While the traditions are old, the adventure is new.

John Wesley wrote a letter to John Trembath in which he advised him: "Whether you like it or no, read and pray daily. It is for your life; there is no other way;…Do justice to your own soul: give it time and means to grow."[2] Perhaps Mary and Joseph deepen their commitment to practicing that care, realizing its importance for their spiritual preparation to receive this special baby. We join them in that concern during our Advent adventure. Just as a baby requires daily time if it is to develop, so it is with our own soul. There are no shortcuts to spiritual growth. We can't merely get interested today, apply the disciplines tomorrow, and the next day it's done! Spirituality is a journey, a process we gradually live into.

Almost without our awareness, however, we get caught up in the secular hype and harried haze of these days. Christmas card signing and stamping. Sales and shopping. Presents and parties. Dinners and decorating. Cookie baking and candy making. Food abounds. Glitz surrounds. Daylight shrinks. Lists lengthen. The secular hype steals the holy silence of the season.

Christmas has become almost universal. However, sometimes it seems to have little to do with the Christian faith or the sacred presence of God in our lives. Those who know nearly nothing about Christianity celebrate the season, embracing the trappings but omitting the Source. The birth of the babe in the stable and the mystery of the power of the manger throughout the centuries have been watered down or lost in the secular world's co-opting of the season. We admit with Isaiah, "We have long been like those whom you do not rule, like those not called by your name" (Isa. 63:19). We know a wistful yearning to recover the spirit and simplicity of that stable night long ago and a soulful hungering for a sense of connectedness with God and one another.

Yet, similar to the way we pack the last box on moving day, we continue to pack one more thing into the season and then one more thing, rushing from activity to activity. Our bodies are here in this place, but our minds are there in the next. Instead of centering ourselves for the day and living through it, being present to each unrelivable moment, we tend to be absentminded to the now, unaware of God's daily gifts, God's sacred space and our place within it.

One day of Advent spins into the next, and suddenly Christmas Eve is upon us. We may discover that, despite our good intentions, we never got around to setting out on our Advent adventure—that "bold undertaking," that "remarkable occurrence," that "stirring experience." The hurry of each day did not allow us time for solitude. Perhaps hurrying itself makes us feel important. Or perhaps we are afraid that, in the words of a secular poet named David Whyte, "slowing for a moment, we might open up the emptiness at the center of all form."[3]

But perhaps this year we will take that risk and turn our backs on the secular hype. Perhaps we will arise in the wee hours of the morning and begin the long drive back home through the holy silence into our empty center, preparing for the baby by tending the void in our own soul. As Patch Adams reminds us in the movie by that name: "All of life is a homecoming."

Sanctuary of the Heart

Scripture: 1 Thessalonians 3:9-13

In *Out to Canaan,* Jan Karon depicts a scene with a little girl named Jessie and the pastor, Father Tim:

> "Look!" said Jessie. "A baby in a box."
>
> She stood on tiptoes, holding her doll, and gazed into the creche that had belonged to his grandmother.
>
> He realized she didn't know about the Babe, and wondered how his life could be so sheltered that he should be surprised.[4]

Jesus is the unknown baby in a box to many children. They know about Christmas—but not about the babe in the manger. He has no place in their lives or the lives of their families.

Suppose that in the beginning, Mary and Joseph do not know they will have to make the trip to Bethlehem before Jesus' birth. Matthew doesn't mention their journey at all, and Luke doesn't tell us how far ahead they knew about it.

Suppose they begin to prepare a place for the baby in their home. That is what parents commonly do. When a baby is coming, we provide a place—a box, a bassinet, a corner of a room, or a whole nursery. But we make sure there is a space. Advent is a time for us to make room for the baby, to prepare a place for him in the sanctuary of our heart.

From the biblical perspective, the heart is the center, the core, the part of us on which the Lord looks. "The Lord does not see as mortals see; they look on the outward appearance, but the Lord looks on the heart" (1 Sam. 16:7). The heart serves as the hub of our feelings, wisdom, discernment, and decisions. It is the site of our grit and transformation. The heart represents the total self, wholeness, holiness. James Fenhagen in *Invitation to Holiness* suggests that the gift of holiness is "the gift of our full humanity."[5] We pray with Paul that God will "strengthen [our] hearts in holiness" (1 Thess. 3:13).

But rather than being spiritually centered, our lives spin out of control. Things run amuck, and we find ourselves racing up the down escalator, wearing ourselves out going nowhere. Renovation is in order if we are to receive the babe in the sanctuary of the heart.

This renovation calls for recognition that communion among

people is a communion of hearts. Indeed, it is a communion of
wounded hearts. All of us are vulnerable in some way. Abba Poeman, an
early desert father whose sayings frequently mention his family, advised, "Teach your heart to keep what your tongue teaches others."[6] In
our communion of hearts, no one is invisible—not the self or the
other. In that communion we honor the opportunities to bless another
in some small way, directly or indirectly; and we also humbly receive
the blessing another offers us. A dynamic synergy arises from the communion of hearts in which one and one do not equal two but, standing side by side, one and one equal eleven (11). And one plus one plus
one, standing together, do not have the power of three but one hundred eleven (111)!

All of us long to belong. Says David Whyte, "Our hope is to stop
the world for one half-second so that we can get on, and perhaps, for
that one precious moment, get a glimpse of a place to which we can
truly belong."[7] What we forget is that each of us can offer a sense of
belonging to the other. Brother David Steindl-Rast tells us that belonging "is *the* basic gift. Every other gift celebrates, in its own way, belonging. Belonging is mutual and all-inclusive."[8]

I witnessed a special sense of belonging when I worshiped with
my son Dirk and daughter-in-law Angela. People from the Blue Peaks
group home sat in the pew in front of us. Though unable to live by
themselves, these folk contributed in some way to society. During
worship they moved about the sanctuary, and during the sermon they
talked to one another up and down the row. But that congregation
welcomed them, ushering them into full belonging—including taking
up the offering. For me, this experience illustrates a community of
faith that seeks not conformity of behavior but communion of hearts.

Renovating the sanctuary of our hearts also calls for recognition
that nothing in our lives is wasted. I remember throwing out the first
one hundred pages of the novel that became my master's thesis in Eng-
lish/creative writing. It took me a long time to realize that those pages
were not a waste of time, that every page and each crossed-out word
were an invisible part of the story—necessary for me to reach the place
where the story I wanted to tell could begin.

So it is in our lives. We could not get *here* without having stepped
there. Even if we feel tossed about by the whims of the waves in the

wind, it has not been wasted. Our entire previous journey enabled us to reach this point, this point where perhaps we will decide to begin the story we really want to live. The essence of our new story includes not only what occurs at high noon but also events in the rising light of dawn and the setting sun of dusk—and even the yeast of failures in the darkness. All are essential in our humble/extraordinary journey. We offer everything up to God. And though, like Adam and Eve we want to run for fig leaves, crouching exposed to God's presence, we discover that instead of shame we may bask in God's grace! In deep gratitude we say with W. H. Auden in his poem "Precious Five": "Bless what there is for being."[9]

Finally, we recognize that we cannot prepare the sanctuary of our hearts by ourselves. Spirituality is not about individualistic willpower; it is about facing toward God.

My husband represented the World Methodist Council at the Lambeth Conference of 1998, a global gathering of Anglican bishops that meets every ten years. During that conference, L'Arche Lambeth community provided a mime performance. A battle between the Blues and the Reds left only two soldiers standing, a Red and a Blue. One had bread to eat; the other had light and heat. But they would not share. Then the angels of mercy came and danced around them, gradually bringing them together. They began to share what they had and to tell each other their stories. In facing each other, they faced God. Their stories continued into the night. When morning came, both acknowledged that it was time to take up their swords again. They tried but could not, for they had shared their stories.

Willpower by itself cannot support a renovation of the heart. In our Reds-versus-Blues, fight-to-the-finish polarization only openness to God's merciful spirit can make the difference. My friend Gloria (one of the busiest people I know and not at all bent toward public piety) put it this way, "I feel I always rest in the arms of God no matter where I am." This kind of trust allows us to sit together and share our stories.

Paul says, "May the Lord be generous in increasing your love and make you love one another and the whole human race" (1 Thess. 3:12, JB). Preparing the sanctuary of our heart for the baby leads to our own transformation. The process of preparation opens our eyes to the possibility of touching others' lives in a more meaningful way—including those, perhaps unnoticed before, who look at the babe in the manger and see only a baby in a box.

Scripture and Spectacle
Scripture: Psalm 80:1-7

Feeling the weight of rearing this baby whom Joseph is to name Jesus, perhaps Mary and Joseph pledge to each other that they will reflect on the Hebrew Scriptures daily and be more aware of seeing the scriptures demonstrated in the lives of others. Our attention to scripture, both through daily reflection and reading it in the lives of others, plays a vital role in our preparation for the baby, just as it does for Mary and Joseph. In *Life Together* Dietrich Bonhoeffer comments on how to read the Bible:

> In our meditation we ponder the chosen text on the strength of the promise that it has something utterly personal to say to us for this day and for our Christian life, that it is not only God's Word for the Church, but also God's Word for us individually....We read God's Word as God's Word for us.[10]

What good intentions we have! But the spectacle of the season drops a veil of distraction over our minds. *yep!*

This veil resembles clouds descending on the mountains. Nothing rises so tall or breaks against the horizon so unshakably and immovably as mountain peaks. Yet airy puffs of clouds, densely gathered, can hide them. The clouds distract our attention; and though we know the peaks exist, we tend to forget about them. Likewise, the quiet whisperings of faith-based essentials in scripture are always there for us, unshakable and immovable. But the clamoring spectacle of market-based nonessentials can affect our focus and distract us. Bowing with Mary and Joseph, we pray with the psalmist, "Restore us, O God; let your face shine, that we may be saved" (Ps. 80:3).

Last year during Advent, our grandson Nathan was scheduled for surgery. I spent a few days with him and my daughter Danna Lee and son-in-love Mark. To brighten the anxiety-ridden night before Nathan entered the hospital, we all took a "light" drive through the city. Christian symbols mixed with secular ones. A heart outlined in Christmas lights stood above the door to a pub. A few blocks down, red chili pepper lights outlined an old mining wagon. One house, however, brought our car to a halt while we stared at the eclectic electric display. Blinking lights framed the windows and twinkled on the trees in the yard. White icicle lights draped the porch, and a huge bell wreath lit the door. Lights of all colors climbed the fence and house to outline the figures of Santa Claus, eight reindeer, an angel, three candles, and a huge sleigh on the roof with Rudolph off to the side. Several manger scenes of various sizes, all plastic and lit, vied for space amidst words that flashed across the yard: *Season's Greetings, MERRY XMAS, Happy New Year.* This is a season of spectacle.

Yet it is also a season when the sound of the scriptures abounds. We hear scriptures read in church Christmas programs, sung in special music, and acted out in living Nativity scenes. A boy from a recently built government housing project noticed commotion in the nearby churchyard. Curious about what was going on, he swaggered over to the other teenagers, his tough-guy posturing intact. They were preparing for a living Nativity. That held no meaning for him; but it looked interesting, so he wanted to be part of the scene.

The church had been searching for a horizontal (rather than vertical) way to connect with the people in the projects, and the opportunity to involve this tough teen elated the youth director. He learned that the boy's name was Mick, and he invited Mick to be a shepherd.

Mick donned the shepherd garb over his clothes, and all the youth took their places in the Nativity. But Mick wasn't interested in focusing on the manger and reenacting the silent simplicity of that night long ago. He had far more fun playing to the cars that drove by, hooting and waving at them.

The youth director finally reached his tolerance level and took Mick aside. He spoke privately but firmly, "Mick, you are not the star of this scene. Jesus is."

"Jesus who?" asked the boy.

Maybe Mick was being flippant. But maybe not; we can't assume that everyone knows who Jesus is. Either way, now Mick knows the answer and can tell the whole story; he's a member of that Dallas church.

Sometimes—if we bother to look (and perhaps during Advent we can look daily)—we see the scriptures enacted in the lives of others. I think of Anglican Archbishop David Gitari of Kenya and his three simple words: "Boil the water!" That's how he begins every single sermon in his country. "Boil the water!" It may not sound as though he's enacting the scriptures, but he is. A major cause of death in Kenya is the waterborne diseases of typhoid, dysentery, and cholera. "Boil the water!" has to do with building a house on the rock, healing through prevention, giving a cup of pure water to the little ones, bringing hope, sowing good seeds, and loving neighbor as oneself. Therefore, through those three vital words Archbishop Gitari enacts much of The Gospel According to Matthew.

One of my friends in the Church of South India is Krupaveni Prakasha Rao, a clergywoman herself and the wife of the Bishop of Krishna-Godavari. Veni told me about a little girl who, while walking down the street with her father, noticed a sign lettered in black. With her elementary English reading skills, the girl's interest in the sign was piqued. The sign actually read, GOD IS NOWHERE. The little girl paused and began to sound out the words one letter at a time: "G-O-D, God. I-S, is. N-O-W, now. H-E-R-E, here." Proud of her achievement, she smiled and said, "God is now here."

As Advent Adventurers, we see both the secular spectacle and the scriptural simplicity of this holy season. We, like that little girl, refuse to conform to the cynicism that "God is nowhere" but allow ourselves to be transformed by the confidence that "God is now here." Though the secular separates itself from the sacred, the sacred encompasses the secular. Teilhard de Chardin affirms that "*nothing* here below *is profane* for those who know how to see. On the contrary, everything is sacred."[11]

Stable Sight

Scripture: 1 Corinthians 1:3-9

Curly-headed little Tommy walked into the entry hall, holding his mother's hand. The crèche was on the table against the wall, just about his height. He stood for a moment beside it, his dark eyes drawn to the babe in the manger and the parents. "Look, Mommy! There's Mary and Joseph and the baby Jesus in his car seat!"

Tommy makes us laugh. Laughter and a sense of playfulness are significant in parenting. Surely Joseph grasps the responsibility of rearing well this child who is to save his people from their sins; and, being a carpenter, he knows the necessity of choosing the right tools for a task. Joseph realizes the seriousness of this mission, but he also understands the importance of play for the child to develop balance and wholeness. As we stand back in the shadows watching Joseph's busy hands, he sets aside his completed work and picks up a small piece of wood. We watch him carefully carve a little toy donkey for the baby.

We have long understood the seriousness of our spiritual adventure, but we can easily overlook the role of playfulness. Brother David advises us, "You can tell true seriousness from glumness by its playfulness. To seek seriously means to seek playfully. And the joyful mysteries of Living by the Word teach us this playfulness."[12] We even may have forgotten how to play. If so, relearning playfulness is a vital aspect of our Advent adventure.

A friend, speaking of playfulness, told me about leading a retreat for a congregation that prides itself on its intellectual and sophisticated self-image. The participants ate dinner, did some business, and had a meditation time. By the time the pastor introduced my friend, it was nearly nine o'clock. "By then," he said, "they were weary and restless. Besides shortening my talk, I used a playful approach to get some energy going. Most of them looked like they were with me. But afterward a couple of women told me my presentation was 'beneath' them. Not 'cerebral' enough." My friend paused, his eyes thoughtful, and added sadly, "Playfulness was so foreign to them that they couldn't board the ship, and so they missed the trip."

Brother David understands that we miss the trip when we lose our playfulness. He mentions that "by far the largest part of the exercises in faith consists of learning God's games. If we insist that God ought to be more serious than that, we'll miss the fun of it all."[13] God sent us a babe in a stable—a babe with smiles and gurgles, thrashing arms and curling toes. Surely then, God intends that our spiritual journey be more than dull duty or merely a "head-trip." God intends that it be a joyful adventure with more than a pinch of playfulness.

Children innately understand that we learn from play. In recent years I have served on the faculty for training new United Methodist district superintendents and conference council directors. This summer we held the final faculty meeting in preparation for their arrival on Sunday morning. We all sat around the tables for worship, including the cute little granddaughter of one of the facilitators. The pastor leading the service began, "Once upon a time there was a man who was beaten and robbed and left by the side of the road." After completing the story of the Good Samaritan, she asked what image came to our minds related to our own lives. As we went around the room, the child took her turn and responded, "Little Red Riding Hood." Her image arose from play. Little Red Riding Hood, like the Good Samaritan, showed care for the one who was ill; and, like the man lying beside the road, she also was saved. Play is an important teacher, even in adulthood.

Children attend seriously to the business of play. Their playfulness can help them through intense situations. I think of a group of children I met in Bosnia. I first saw them outside in a small dirt yard behind their overcrowded refugee center, a building pocked with bullet holes. Hand-washed laundry hung in the corner of the yard, draped without clothespins on a rope stretched between a shack and a wood fence with missing planks. These children knew the cruelties of war, the panic of bullet-riddled and bombed-out homes, the pain of losing loved ones. Even in that moment we could hear the sound of shelling in the distance. Yet they gathered together and played with a cat they'd found, their laughter ringing in the late afternoon sun.

Through stable sight and insight we rediscover the joy of playfulness that can come when we seriously seek the One who will "strengthen [us] to the end" (1 Cor. 1:8). Risking adventure during Advent, we pack up the baby Jesus "in his car seat" and take him with us in the stable site of our hearts, bowing in awe to the loving Holy One who is present in the distant and cosmic—yet somehow is also present in the close and the common.

Sleeping and Waking
Scripture: Romans 13:11-14

Tommy's remark in the previous section reminds us not only of the importance of playfulness but also of the need to integrate theology into our lives. Instead of separating theology from his young world, Tommy practiced it by connecting the life of Jesus to his own familiar days, just as Jesus connected his teachings to the ordinary lives and everyday work of the people. We live the faith by envisioning Christ's life in relationship to our own culture and by trying daily to emulate what we see.

Though Mary and Joseph obviously do not have Christ's life to emulate while they prepare for his birth, they know the Hebrew Scriptures. Like us, they know of God's presence in the journey and God's power to help us live more faithfully and fully. Perhaps they understand that only as they become fully alive can they teach this special child how to live fully himself. Neither they nor we can prepare well for the baby if we sleepwalk through Advent. C. S. Lewis in *Letters to Malcolm* says,

> We may ignore, but we can nowhere evade, the presence of God. The world is crowded with [God]. [God] walks everywhere *incognito*. And the *incognito* is not always hard to penetrate. The real labour is to remember, to attend. In fact, to come awake. Still more, to remain awake.[14]

Paul expresses concern and tells us "to wake from sleep" (Rom. 13:11).

Just as Lent provides a time for wandering in the wilderness to prepare for Christ's crucifixion and life *after* death, the Advent adventure prepares us for Christ's birth and life *before* death. In *The Rule of Benedict*, Joan D. Chittister, O.S.B., tells the story of an ancient seeker and his teacher. When the seeker asks whether there is life after death, the teacher responds, "The great spiritual question of life is not, 'Is there life after death?' The great spiritual question is, 'Is there life before death?'"[15] As Advent Adventurers, we journey toward full living.

Brother David states "that you have not yet died is not sufficient proof that you're alive. Aliveness is measured by degrees of awareness."[16] In this moment, the future is fantasy and the past is memory; the present is the present to unwrap today. As we grow in awareness of God's presence in *this* moment, we begin to see the daily gifts that went unnoticed before. We awaken to the extra in the ordinary—the tiny droplets glistening on the white petals of the African violet, the mottled hand of the elderly hospital volunteer reaching out in tender care, the smile in the voice of a small grandchild saying on the phone, "Ch'ismas coming!" We begin to anticipate surprise—the unexpected gift from God's good earth, the accidental moments with another, the unpredicted incident that can warm our hearts. We become more aware of the Creator in all of creation, seeing with our ears and listening with our eyes, sensing the unsaid in the silence and touching the other with a glance.

Without awareness of God's presence, life can feel like an endurance test. Escape may seem the only way to know life more fully—escape from job, neighborhood, community, or economic conditions. Or escape from the people around us—friends, spouse, colleagues. To some degree we resemble Ada in the novel *Cold Mountain* by Charles Frazier. Although Ada needs to sell off things to survive financially, she clings to the cabriolet, a two-wheeled, one-horse carriage:

> It was the mobility of the thing that held her to it. The promise in its tall wheels that if things got bad enough she could just climb in and ride away…and take the attitude that there was no burden that couldn't be lightened, no wreckful life that couldn't be set right by heading off down the road.[17]

External changes are necessary sometimes. Yet after making them we may find ourselves living no more fully than before. Being *alive* rarely depends upon, nor is guaranteed by, changing our situation.

Awareness of God's presence in the tough times may foster a change in our attitude toward the situation and, thereby, change our style of living within it. Going to parenting classes with Mary and Joseph reminds us that we have to deal with the difficulties that arise. All babies are a challenge sometimes! But we don't climb up on the cabriolet and escape. We stick it out—through colic and crying, fever and fits, disruption and diapers. We are there for the duration.

Hispanic culture offers an important teaching with regard to suffering: Suffering is not something to run away from but something to honor. Practicing theology gradually builds our confidence so we can tote our burdens of suffering to the other side—not so much getting through them as growing through them. We don't need a cabriolet! Healing our hearts is an important aspect of life after birth. We grow spiritually by rejoicing in the happy times and sticking it out during the difficult ones. Paul says, "I have learned, in whatsoever state I am, therewith to be content. I know both how to be abased, and I know how to abound" (Phil. 4:11-12, KJV).

A story from the Hasidim tells about a preacher who repeatedly admonished, "Put God into your life." The village rabbi proposed a different perspective, suggesting that our task is not to put God into our lives, because God is already there; our task is simply to realize that God is present.[18]

God is present with us whether we are in the pits or on the pedestal. Becoming awake to that presence is like swirling a kaleidoscope and watching the drab fragments of our lives dance into new patterns of possibility that offer us *life* before death.

Solstice and Shadows

Scripture: Isaiah 2:1-5

Fear filled the voice of my little granddaughter Chelsea as we spoke on the phone in the late afternoon darkness of this December day. "I don't like the dark!"

I wanted to wrap my arms around her and hold her on my lap. But across the miles I could only hug her with my words and tone of voice. "Sweetheart, every single night passes into morning. God *always* brings the light."

After a moment of silence Chelsea said, "God loves us. God chases the monsters away."

The days grow shorter and shorter as we approach the winter solstice, and we spend more and more time in darkness. Many of us leave for our jobs and also return in the dark, and in our windowless work places we do not see the sunlight at all. The dark night of the soul can fall upon us, shutting down our senses. We go through the motions of living, and our eager anticipation of the Christmas babe ebbs in the waves of darkness.

Perhaps Joseph or Mary also experience the dark night of the soul at some point while awaiting the baby's birth. Neither Matthew's narration of Joseph's dream nor Luke's appearance of the angel to Mary includes a guaranteed end to the dark night of the human soul or to the shadows of darkness in the world's soul. We can imagine Joseph bent over to work with wood while his mind wanders to the baby and the grave concern of helping him grow in stature and spirit, wisdom and grace. Perhaps Joseph dreads the difficulties of rearing this child in such a troubled world—a world of political turmoil, vast economic in-equalities, and human atrocities (like many parents-to-be feel today). We can also imagine Mary's mind wandering as she draws water from the well, pondering how her son will one day turn the world topsy-turvy by bringing down the powerful and lifting up the lowly. For an instant a frown of fear for him creases her young brow. Mary and Joseph's assurance for this baby is the baby himself, for Joseph is to name him Jesus—"God is with us." Even in the darkness.

As we look back over these 2,000 years, we know that the dark night of the human soul and the dark shadows of the world's soul continue. Our confidence, like that of Mary and Joseph, rests in the trust that *God is with us* through all our dark nights. Preparing to care for the baby teaches us how to deal with those dark times, for regardless of what is going on within us and around us, we must care for a baby when a baby needs care. In spite of our mood or our weariness or our groping our way through the dark night of the soul, if the baby cries out we must get up in the darkness and stumble to the cradle. So too do we care for our life in the spirit. Even in the dark night of the soul we stumble toward the manger, and we learn what we did not know we knew about ourselves: We are loved by God; and when we face the dark pool sucking us downward, God's presence can help chase away the monsters lurking there.

But what of the monsters that live not in the dream world but in the day world? Those monsters who make news headlines that we keep at a distance because of the horror of the atrocities—until a face we know shares the story firsthand. Then it all comes to life, and we cannot hide.

Eleanor Gbonda, wife of the Bishop of Bo in Sierra Leone, has become a dear friend. At the Lambeth Conference, spouses met in small groups for daily Bible study, and we were in the same one. Eleanor is a courageous woman who helped save her compound from the soldiers. The tears come when she speaks about her country's troubles. And I cannot forget her dark eyes that look into the distance and see the scenes again, nor her resonant voice as she prays, nor that final shrug as she affirms her trust: "We leave it to God."

Nor can I forget the monsters of Sierra Leone. They send living letters of terror by hacking off children's hands, arms, and feet, and gouging out their eyes. They mutilate civilian men and also women, targeting pregnant ones. So many victims! A young man still shakes when he describes the monsters chopping off his arms and repeats over and over again his powerlessness now, even to go to the bathroom without help. A youth stares hopelessly at two stumps where his feet used to be. A little boy's last memory of sight before eyeless darkness is the monster coming toward his face. Still echoing in a little girl's mind are her screams of terror as she watches a monster draw back his arm and hack off her mother's hand, and then he bends and chops off hers. The monsters come once to mutilate, and they come over and over again in their victims' nightmares. What does a grandparent say to a child in Sierra Leone who is afraid of the dark?

How do we comfort the children who suffer because of the dark shadows of the world's soul? The children in the war-torn countries of Africa. Or the precarious Balkans. Or the starving children of Sudan. Or the victims of bombs that maim from a distance. We shake in anger, paralyzed by confusion and our own powerlessness, longing desperately for this kind of night to pass into morning. We cry out for God to chase these monsters away!

Suppose that little girl without a hand or that footless boy were my child or grandchild. How could I forgive the monsters? Why would I even try? Wouldn't I hunger for revenge, for the same thing exactly— or worse—to befall the monsters? But then where would vengeance and countervengeance end? Would they, like violence in the Balkans, go on for centuries?

> "You have heard that it was said, 'An eye for an eye and a tooth for a tooth.' But now I tell you: do not take revenge on someone who wrongs you....You have heard that it was said, 'Love your friends, hate your enemies.' But now I tell you: love your enemies and pray for those who persecute you" (Matt. 5:38-39, 43-44, TEV).

This is the One for whom we prepare! This radical One who says what we do not want to hear! Who grates against our instincts. Who turns vengeance into love.

We argue with that teaching. Look where it got him! Could the horrors of Hitler have been stopped without force? Rigid, simplistic answers do not fit a complex world! Yet in the bedlam, a tiny voice whispers, wondering if Christians standing together around the globe could have brought the light and prevented the Holocaust. If Christians had been informed, had united globally from the beginning, had remained faithful to the teachings of Christ, and had found the needed courage, could history have been written differently? Could it be written differently today? Isaiah calls to us, "Come, let us go up to the mountain of the Lord" (Isa. 2:3). From that mountaintop perhaps we could learn to see through the eyes of unity and to demonstrate the wisdom of our faith and to grow in the courage to carry God's light into the dark shadows.

According to historian John Higham at Johns Hopkins University, when we look back in time we find that after each major war in which the United States participated, the country reworked its approach to racism.[19] These major traumas led to a social shift—if ever so small—that resulted in progressive change. Could Higham be right? If so, could we generalize to other changes? And if so, could national truth also be global truth? For example, we can point to new international sensitivity regarding anti-Semitism following World War II. Looking back, we see hope in the hearts of people and, therefore, perhaps infinitesimally in history itself. How I long for this to be so!

In *Lord of the Dance* by Andrew M. Greeley, Ace and Danny talk:

> "But that's what it's about," Ace said. "Christmas is the surprise of light coming back, Easter the surprise of spring returning. Our faith is the ability to be open to surprises."[20]

During the darkest days of winter in our own soul and in the soul of the world, Advent's surprise of returning light draws us. We rediscover that God loves us and never gives up on us. Even in the darkness, "God is with us."

Stirrings of the Soul

Scripture: Psalm 25:1-10

In our mind's eye we see Mary lean down and unlatch a trunk lid. She moves things aside, and toward the bottom she finds the scrapbook-scroll of highlights from her own childhood. She sits down to rest. We watch over her shoulder as she unrolls the scroll, distant soul-stirring memories coming alive. She knows that revisiting her own memories will help her understand what to do and what not to do in making memories for her son.

Our own soul-stirring memories come alive as we begin to "deck the halls" for the Christmas season. The decorations prompt recollection—re-collection—of past scenes in our lives. They help us see the world within us more clearly and the world around us more compassionately.

I especially enjoy getting out the striped Christmas stockings in red, green, and white that I've knitted over the years, adding new ones as spouses and grandchildren join our family. The one lone sock of our first child now hangs among an even dozen, two of which that grown child knitted—one for Bill and one for me. I stand back to look at the stockings crowded together across the mantel and feel myself smile, my heart warmed. Seeing the name on each stocking is like hearing a roll call with all the family members answering "Present." Though I am alone, it seems as though they are with me in the room.

When I unbox the Christmas wreath and hang it on the front door, I think of Judy and Franklin, treasured friends who gave us the wreath long ago. Deciding to put some action behind my thoughts, I call them and we reconnect across the miles.

Next come the Dickens carolers, given to us, one each Christmas, by the church staff in Enid, Oklahoma. I set them out, remembering our special times in that church, the one Bill was serving when he was elected and consecrated a bishop. Getting out Christmas decorations each year is like hanging a tapestry that depicts our memories of family, good friends, and high moments in our spiritual adventure.

Many families have a tradition of gathering together to put up the Christmas tree. Draping the lights from limb to limb. Pulling out the old ornaments. Pausing with each one and remembering the friend who gave it or the child who made it. At our house we place an angel on the very top, shabby now like the Velveteen Rabbit, for it has reigned over our tree since Bill and I first married. Finally comes that annual moment in many households of turning on the lights for the first time. The room is darkened. Everyone grows silent in expectation. And suddenly, *magic*! The tree dances with light! Perhaps popcorn or pizza is eaten around the tree, delight abounding. And another memory is made.

Some of us have a storehouse of wonderful childhood memories that helped us develop a sense of expectancy and excitement and wonder in this season, especially Christmas Eve and Christmas Day. Church family gathered around the altar table for Christmas Eve Communion. Immediate and extended family gathered around the home table, a table loaded with favorite holiday foods. Traditional sounds and sights enhanced the background. The giving and receiving of gifts added to the joy.

All of these remembrances bring gratitude that wells up from the deepest part of us and overflows. In that fullness we pray with the psalmist, "To you, O Lord, I lift up my soul" (Ps. 25:1).

Our Advent adventure is not just about the recesses of our minds but also about the crevices of our world, those places where we hide what we do not wish to see. There are those people who cannot deck the halls—their institutional halls. There are those who have no socks to wear—let alone to hang. There are those who have no family—having lost them for various reasons along the way. There are those who shiver from the cold—whose hearts are never warmed. There are those who cannot read—not Dickens or the Bible; those who've heard no carolers—nor even heard of them; and those whose collections consist of soda cans—put in a trash bag and sold for survival. There are those who have no bed, walls, or door—let alone a wreath to place upon it. There are those who have forgotten the faces of their friends—and have been forgotten by them. There are those without custom or continuity—except for the unbroken darkness around and within them. And there are those without milk to drink or bread to eat—let alone pizza around a Christmas tree magically alit. Henri J. M. Nouwen in *Bread for the Journey* says that "everything within and around us conspires to make us ignore, avoid, suppress, or simply deny these sorrows."[21]

Even for many people who live in comfort, Christmas memories that stir the soul are predominantly unhappy ones. A sense of dread envelops the season as past childhood scenes of disappointment, drunkenness, or violence on Christmas and Christmas Eve come to mind, for their parents acted out of their own painful childhood memories. We seem to hand down behavior patterns just as we hand down the china

and the old rocking chair. Some of these persons now dream of a Hall-
mark Christmas for their family but find themselves continuing those
same destructive patterns. Others have been able to reform—re-form—
the generation-to-generation patterns, making good memories for
their children.

Nouwen speaks of "not avoiding but befriending our sorrows."[22]
Our Advent adventure includes a creative reviewing—re-viewing—of
those unhappy scenes. This venture into the past does not suggest re-
pression of those painful memories. Instead, it encourages a process of
pulling them shyly from the shadows and setting them softly in the
light. We entrust them to the loving Holy One who can bless us with
the power to forgive those who scarred us and give us a new perspective so we don't continue the pattern of scarring. In this hope we pray
with the psalmist, "O my God, in you I trust; do not let me be put to
shame; do not let my enemies [those inner enemies, O Lord] exult
over me" (Ps. 25:2).

Christmas memories become a special blessing when a loved one
dies. In *Out to Canaan*, Father Tim reaches up on the closet shelf and
happens to touch the box of mementos of his dead mother:

> The handkerchiefs, her wedding ring, an evening purse, buttons...
>
> He stood there, not seeing the box with his eyes, but in his
> memory. It was covered with wallpaper from their dining room in
> Holly Springs a half century, an eon, ago. Cream colored roses
> with pale green leaves...
>
> He would not take it down, but it had somehow released mem-
> ories of his mother's Christmases, and the scent of chickory coffee
> and steaming puddings and cookies baking on great sheets;...and
> the guest room with its swirl of gifts and carefully selected sur-
> prises, tied with the signature white satin ribbon.
>
> Father Tim's fingers lingered on the box: "Mother..." he whis-
> pered into the darkened warmth of the closet. "I remember...."[23]

Yes, all of us remember a loved one now absent from the table. And we
pray with the psalmist, "All the paths of the Lord are steadfast love and
faithfulness" (Ps. 25:10).

This season of soul-stirring memories offers us an opportunity to
recollect, review, and reform inherited patterns that have shaped us;

and to do so in a way that celebrates the past, clarifies the present, and calls us toward an open future.

✦

Traditionally, Advent is a liturgical season of preparation for the birth of the Christ child in the world and in our lives. It invites celebration and an entangled adventure toward spiritual renewal. In *Cold Mountain*, Inman journeys toward home:

> He had learned enough of books to think that gravity in its ideal form was supposed to work in straight lines of force. But looking on the creek as it made its snaky way down the hill, he saw such notions to be just airy thoughts. The creek's turnings marked how all that moves must shape itself to the maze of actual landscape, no matter what its preferences might be.[24]

So it is with our spiritual journey. Regardless of our preferences and fantasies, we make this journey by traveling through our own unique and individual landscape mazes, which include paths to contend with and paths to celebrate, varying continually in light and terrain. Our attempt to recover the stable and to restore simplicity and serenity to the hectic Advent season calls for a realistic look at our landscape and for discipline, changed habits, and a new style of moving toward Christmas within that landscape. But this we know: God is present on the journey, and our unceasing awareness of that Presence makes all the difference along the way.

THOUGHTS AND REFLECTIONS

✧ When did you most feel the presence of God this week? When did you least feel the presence of God this week?

✧ Think about what it would mean to take your Advent adventure seriously. What risks would it bring?

✧ Name some of the things already on your calendar during the Advent season. Which activities foster your preparation for the rebirth of Christ in your life? Which block your preparation? How could setting a time each day for focusing on your spiritual growth during this season help you prepare for new life in the Spirit?

✧ Contemplate the sanctuary of the heart. What renovation does yours need?

✧ Think about the secular spectacle of the season and its scriptural simplicity; compare the two.

✧ While understanding the significance of seriousness in your spiritual journey, do you oftentimes overlook the role of playfulness? How is playfulness a part of your spiritual adventure? If you can envision taking "the baby Jesus in his car seat" with you wherever you go, how might that change your attitude and actions?

✧ Think about what it means to have life *before* death. How does your awareness of God's presence enhance your daily living? What changes within you might improve some of the troublesome situations in your life?

✧ Consider a dark night of the soul you have experienced. Share your experience of the surprise of light coming back.

✧ What is one Christmas memory that brings you joy? What can you do to give a joyous Christmas memory during this Advent season to someone who might not have one otherwise?

Rekindling the Sacred

GEORGIA O'KEEFFE entitled one of her paintings *Dry Waterfall*. It speaks mutedly and powerfully through its steep cliffs and the chasm dividing them. To me, it speaks of meaning. When we seek meaning where true meaning cannot be found, the cliffs and chasms of our lives form dry waterfalls. When we feel disconnected from our Creator and void of reverence, the fire of the Spirit turns to ashes, and the waters of the soul dry up.

Advent offers us signs that point toward rekindling the sacred. To *kindle* is to "set on fire, inspire, light, animate." *Sacred* relates to being connected to the Creator; it evokes a sense of reverence. As the baby's birth draws near, the signs of Advent appear. A spark glows in the ashes. Howard Thurman's words from *The Inward Journey* fall gently like snow in the moonlight, calling us to "sensitize our spirits...that we may tread reverently in the common way."[1] We begin to find God where we could not see God before.

Renewing Our Baptism

Scripture: Mark 1:1-8

Angels are one of the signs of the season that point toward rekindling the sacred. In the first chapter of Matthew an angel appears to Joseph and says, "Do not be afraid." In the first two chapters of Luke, an angel comes to Zechariah and states: "Do not be afraid," to Mary: "Do not be afraid," and to the shepherds: "Do not be afraid." The angels bring two messages: Life is going to be different in some significant way, and "Do not be afraid."

John said, "I have baptized you with water; but he will baptize you with the Holy Spirit" (Mark 1:8). One of my Louisiana friends, knowing that the church school lesson had been on Jesus' baptism, asked her granddaughter during Sunday dinner what she'd learned that morning. The five-year-old replied, "Jesus was baptized by his best friend." Bright-eyed and confident, she added, "In the bayou."

We chuckle, and yet Louisiana bayous are like our faith journey, twisting and slow moving. They are filled with sly alligators and steadfast cypress trees draped in Spanish moss. The bayous, like our baptism, offer both risk and tranquility. During this season of faith and frenzy, we would welcome the latter, but we don't want the concomitant risks. Pericles spoke of courage: "Those who can most truly be accounted brave are those who know the meaning of what is sweet in life and what is terrible, and then go out, undeterred, to meet what is to come."[2]

One way we rekindle the sacred is by renewing our baptism. Yet we hesitate, knowing that if we renew it and begin to take baptism seriously, our life will be different in some significant way; and we have difficulty trusting the message, "Do not be afraid." Our religion can become like that of Hubert in *A Certain Justice* by P. D. James:

> The practice of his religion, which, it seemed to him now, had never been more than a formal affirmation of a received set of values, was now little more than a pointless exercise designed to give shape to the week. The wonder, the mystery, the sense of history— all had gone.[3]

The Methodist Children's Home in Waco, Texas, has an annual Christmas party that a particular family has sponsored for many decades. The small children now represent the fifth generation. Everyone gathers in the gym for a program, followed by bounteous fruit and candy gifts. My participation in the giving is an experience that brings both pleasure and pain. The children and youth pass from table to table to receive their treats. I give my name and invite theirs, wanting to establish eye contact with each one, hoping to connect person-to-person during this millisecond Christmas encounter with each child. It is not easy. These children reside here because their lives have been difficult. Many of them hide behind thick walls of stone, pretending to be invisible. Often their growth toward self-worth and value has been stunted. They do not know they are God's precious children. Some have forgotten. Others have never been told.

How can we bless others with that good news if we doubt it about ourselves? How can we bless others if we never change our scenery to include them? Recently while in New York, I saw the play *The Diary of Anne Frank*. We all know the story. The Frank family and four other Jews lived in hiding in a storage area above a business. They had been there for six months when the stage lights dimmed for intermission. As I walked downstairs, I heard a conversation between a girl around age ten and her father. "Do you think they will change the scenery?" she asked. After a pause her father responded in that teaching-moment tone all parents use at times: "Do you think the Frank family got to change scenery?"

The Franks' scenery was forced, but we make a choice. We tend to remain in our self-imposed hiding place, fearful and stagnant, coming out occasionally to pose for religious photo-ops. Borrowing a line from T. S. Eliot's poem "The Dry Salvages," we settle for "only a shell, a husk of meaning."[4]

Our Advent adventure calls us to renew our baptism; to say yes to risk during times of tranquility and yes to tranquility during times of risk; to bow to the way of the water and the cosmic rhythm of the river, for as Teilhard de Chardin reminds us: "The Christian's life is a continuous building and a fragmenting and a coming apart in order to come together again less centered on self and more centered on Jesus Christ."[5] If we renew the dance of baptism, life is going to be different in some significant way. But we need not be afraid, for we will dance in the sacred stillness of communion with the Creator.

Reawakening Our Sense of Holiness
Scripture: Luke 3:1-6

The shepherds also signal the season, pointing us to rekindle the sacred by recognizing that holiness is not reserved for pope and prelates. God's presence with the common folk is notable in Luke. We see it when the shepherds hear the angel and follow what they hear. We also see it in the next chapter, for Luke speaks of the rulers: "In the fifteenth year of the reign of Emperor Tiberius, when Pontius Pilate was governor of Judea, and Herod was ruler of Galilee, and his brother Philip ruler of the region of Ituraea and Trachonitis, and Lysanias ruler of Abilene" (Luke 3:1). Then he mentions the high priests by name: "during the high priesthood of Annas and Caiaphas" (Luke 3:2). Finally he gets to the point: "The word of God came to John in the wilderness" (Luke 3:2). The word of God comes not to an emperor, not to a high priest—but to John. And it comes not in the Roman forum, not in the synagogue—but in the wilderness. *aren't we all in the wilderness?*

Brother David suggests that what matters is not "knowledge *about* God, but knowledge *of* God—as the magnetic North of the human heart."[6] To reawaken our sense of holiness is to direct our heart toward God. When we do this, nothing changes—yet everything changes.

I know of a woman perpetually prepared for the Christmas season. Cut into her den wall is a door that opens into a large closet in her garage. A few weeks before Christmas, she simply opens that wide pocket door in her den; and there before her stands the front half of a Christmas tree, in place and permanently decorated. She's ready! No struggle to set up the tree or drape the lights or touch the ornaments that trigger memories or space the icicles. Just open the door, and presto! A tree facade appears, fully adorned!

Ah, if holiness were only so simple! Just offer up a facade, half a self, a closed-off existence unexposed to changing realities. But holiness is a process that holds its course to the magnetic north, a bold and open journey beyond artifice, yet capable of encompassing it. As we reawaken our sense of holiness, we learn how to see all of God's creation as sacred space. Or is it that as we learn how to see all of God's creation as sacred space, we reawaken our sense of holiness? Chittister states,

> Holiness is in the Now but we go through life only half conscious

of it, asleep or intent on being someplace other than where we are. We need to open our eyes and see things as they exist around us: what is valuable and what is not, what enriches and what does not, what is of God and what is not.[7]

Perhaps all of us have known stages when nothing seemed valuable or enriching. Our reluctant feet touched the floor each morning, and we began pacing the dungeon with the living dead. We have also known moments when we have experienced joy so dazzling and a sense of holiness so radiant that we raised a hand to our brow to shield our eyes. Those moments are rare and extraordinary; if we expect them to become commonplace, we will be disappointed. As we become more conscious of holiness, it is not that this sense of radiance becomes common, but that in the common we begin to see God's radiance, a radiance there for us even in the dungeon.

In *A Tree Full of Angels*, Macrina Wiederkehr suggests that "everything in your life is a stepping-stone to holiness if only you recognize that you do have within you the grace to be present to each moment."[8] This cognizance is part of the mystery of the manger. The daily gifts are always there. Advent can teach us to *see* them. David Whyte says the "simple ability to pay attention to the world as we find it may be at the heart of a soulful life worth living."[9]

Allan Houser (anglicized from his Native American name Ha-o-zous) was a Chiricahua Apache sculptor whose father rode with Geronimo. Houser was awarded the National Medal of the Arts in 1992. He died two years later, but his presence continues through his sculptures that are scattered all around the world. Every piece speaks in the native language of each admirer. His bronze *Sacred Rain Arrow* speaks to me of power, but his *Shy One* speaks to me of holiness. Ha-o-zous would look at a stone and get in touch with its longings, with what it wanted to become, always seeking "that great simplicity, that elimination of everything that doesn't really need to be interpreted."[10] In *Shy One* he sculpted a Native American child leaning in toward her mother who holds her hand. Only their faces and heights distinguish them. The blankets around their shoulders merge and their long dresses flow so softly together that the hard coldness of the sculpture comes as a surprise.

Holiness is that great simplicity, our elimination of everything that doesn't really need to be there. A sense of holiness helps us get in touch with the stone of our life and what it wants to become. It frees us from the armor of competitiveness and intimidation, dressing us in gentle strength born of deep confidence in the Holy One. A sense of holiness brings a warmth to coldness and a softness to the hard world that lies beyond us and sometimes within us. We lean in toward the omniscient, all-powerful God who gently takes our hand.

Reconsidering Our Mind-Set
Scripture: Isaiah 11:1-10

Another sign of Advent that points to rekindling the sacred is the appearance of the heavenly host with the angel, "singing praises to God, 'Glory to God in the highest heaven,'" (Luke 2:14, TEV). Songs of praise become one of the joys of this season. We sing familiar carols, listen to beautiful choirs, and hear the children sing. In their white robes with wide bows at the neck, they look like cherubs and sing like angels. We fantasize Isaiah looking at such a sight as this when he proclaimed, "A little child shall lead them" (Isa. 11:6).

I experienced being led by a little child when my granddaughter Chelsea, three at the time, asked me to play Candyland with her. I landed on a square that required me to stay there until I drew a yellow card. She solved my problem simply—she fingered through the stack of cards until she found a yellow one. "Here, Grandmom," she said, handing it to me. "Now you can move." Later she drew the card that allowed her to cross into the castle and win, but instead she swooped back to my blue gingerbread boy and scooted it along with her red one. "See, Grandmom. We can both win."

As adults, when we look back and see another person stuck along life's journey, what are our reactions and actions? Are we just relieved that we're not stuck? Do we feel a bit smug about our own ability to keep moving? Do we flip mentally through the stack of options and try to find one that will help the other move forward again? Or do we race on toward the goal, gleefully competitive? When we are about to "win," do we ever scoop up the other and hold hands across the goal line? What do our responses say, if anything, about our concept of God? about promoting peace on earth?

When Chelsea and I played our game, she—typical of small children—led from a mind-set of abundance rather than scarcity. As adults our possessions so possess us that even the words *scarcity* and *abundance* bring material things to mind. But the scarcity-abundance dichotomy reaches deeper. It intrigues me because I've come to believe that it strongly influences us without our even realizing it.

All of us experience difficult stages when we tote the heavy burden of despondency, and a sense of abundance eludes us. Frazier (*Cold Mountain*) portrays this through the eyes of Inman, a wounded soldier trying to make his way home during the Civil War. Looking through a pamphlet, Inman notices the last heading, "Graham Flour: Pathway to the More Abundant Life."

> He said it aloud. Pathway to the More Abundant Life.
> —It's what many seek, the woman said. But I'm not sure a sack of flour will set your foot on it.
> —Yes, Inman said. Abundance did seem, in his experience, to be an elusive thing. Unless you counted plenty of hardship. There was ample of that. But abundance of something a man might want was a different matter.
> —Scarcity's much more the general bearing of life, is the way I see it, the woman said.
> —Yes, Inman said.[11]

This expectation of scarcity is common when we find ourselves slogging through difficulties. However, during normal times we can learn a lot about ourselves by developing an awareness of our habitual responses to others and to our surroundings.

I am grateful to Henri J. M. Nouwen (*Bread for the Journey*) and Parker J. Palmer (*The Active Life*) for their ideas on scarcity and abundance. Both of them base their notions on the story of the loaves and fishes. Nouwen speaks of a "scarcity mentality" that "involves hoarding whatever we have, fearful that we won't have enough to survive." He says, "God is a god of abundance, not a god of scarcity....God doesn't give us just enough. God gives us more than enough: more bread and fish than we can eat, more love than we dared to ask for." He adds, "When we live with this mind-set, we will see the miracle that what we give away multiplies: food, knowledge, love...everything. There will even be many leftovers."[12]

A mind-set of scarcity or abundance can permeate our perceptions. Either one may become a self-fulfilling prophecy that tends to produce whatever we expected. For example, with a mind-set of abundance we share our bits of bread and fish, resulting in plenty. With a mind-set of scarcity we hoard them, resulting in paucity. I recall the run on low-fat fudge cookies when they first came out several years ago. As soon as they hit the shelves, they were gone—because people like me bought four boxes instead of one. Fearing scarcity we hoarded. And in the hoarding, we created the very scarcity we feared.

Marketers use this dynamic adroitly. A classic example occurs this time of year when they name and promote *the toy* as though every child in the U.S.—Christian or otherwise—*must* get one for Christmas or is surely deprived and unloved! The media reports daily the scarcity of *the toy*.

A mind-set of scarcity also affects the intangible aspects of life. When we look through the lens of scarcity, we tend to compete for respect, prestige, honor—as though they exist in limited quantity. And they become so. But boldly confident in life abundant, we can share them; and they abound. People may view even love and kindness as scarce commodities to hide under the mattress rather than to share. Hidden away, they cannot be given and multiplied, and they do indeed become scarce.

Fear is both a motivator of scarcity and its reaction. In *A Simpler Way*, Margaret J. Wheatley and Myron Kellner-Rogers describe our destructive confusion, saying that "we believe that fear is the primary motivator for change, that people change only when they are scared. We bully one another into new behaviors by telling terrifying tales of the forces that threaten us."[13] They go on to state,

> Fearing people, we control one another mercilessly. Fearing change, we choose our little plans over the surprise of emergence. …After so many years of defending ourselves against life and searching for better controls, we sit exhausted in the unyielding structures of organization we've created, wondering what happened. What happened to effectiveness, to creativity, to meaning? What happened to us?[14]

No wonder, according to Brother David, the most often repeated commandment in the Bible is "Fear not!—Be not afraid!"[15]

Cardinal Basil Hume tells how his image of God shifted one day when as a small boy, he and his siblings received stern admonishment from their mother to stay out of the cookie jar. She concluded with the sanction, "And remember! God is watching!" From that moment forward he saw God no longer as the One who could be trusted completely, but as the One who watched for his every fault. For decades he held this attitude. Here Hume relates the conclusion of his story:

> One day…I received a very special grace that completely changed my attitude toward God. I realized that if as a child I had put my hand in the cookie jar, and if it had been between meals, and if God had really been watching me, [God] would have said, "Son, why don't you take another one?"[16]

Is our own image of God more like one who guards the cookie jar or one who offers a second cookie? Is our image of God more like a judge we can bribe or a giver of grace and love? Does our image of God more closely resemble one who accuses or one who affirms? Do we tend to see God's gifts as paltry or plentiful? Do we primarily distrust God or trust God? Do we feel afraid of God or loved by God? Are we inclined to perceive God reaching out to us in hostility or in hospitality? Our habitual responses, better than our words, reveal our attitude toward God.

More than we realize, we have a choice about these habitual responses. It takes a while to become aware of them and even longer to change them. But ultimately we do not have to hunker down in scarcity. We can *learn* to look out at the world with the clarity of a pre-sanctioned child, rejoicing in the babe in the manger who helps us cut through our fear-born chains and shows us the mystery of abundant life. Rekindling the sacred, we join our voices with the heavenly host, "praising God and singing: 'Glory to God in the highest heaven'" (Luke 2:13-14, JB).

Responding with Gratefulness

Scripture: Psalm 96

The gifts of the magi are a sign of the season that points to rekindling the sacred through gratefulness. When gratitude becomes a habitual response to life, we are thrice-blessed: blessed with awareness of the amazing experience of life, blessed with a wholehearted feeling of gratefulness that floods up within us, and blessed by the joy of expressing our gratitude. We sing with the psalmist:

> Let the heavens be glad, and let the earth rejoice;
> let the sea roar, and all that fills it;
> let the field exult, and everything in it (Ps. 96:11).

Each morning when I sit down at the desk in my study nook to begin writing, I receive an amazing gift. To some it would be simple technology. To me it is a miracle. I flip on the computer and the precious voices of Chelsea and Sarah, my two little granddaughters who live far away, tell me, "Good morning, Grandmom." A giggle follows. And my writing time begins with a smile and deep joy. Later when I finish—whether I've written a few sentences worth saving or simply filled the wastebasket with wrinkled wads of paper—I hear a wondrous word of grace as I turn off the computer, "We love you, Grandmom." That enduring gift brings delight.

Children know delight. They experience it even in the smallest things. I remember taking our two-year-old grandson Nathan for a walk. Every few steps he would stop, squat, and stare fascinated for long moments at a tiny bug in the grass or a small wildflower that caught his attention. Little ones' eyes light up in appreciation as they see the gifts that abound in nature and people, gifts unnoticed by adults in our harried, self-imposed blindness. Ah, to regain that sense of gratefulness—great-fullness! That delight in life abundant.

In our busy adult world we do not savor life. The entire Advent season can go by without our looking up once at the night sky. We don't see the stars like twinkling Christmas lights flung across the dome above and the sliver of moon like a swing in the sky. We don't enjoy the carolers huddled together and singing on our doorstep, for we're hurrying to move out the door ourselves and on to something else. We don't watch the white flakes whirling into patterns on the branches pulled like drapes across the lane. Or hear the scrunch of boots in the snow. Or smell the bread or taste the grapes. In our lack of savoring, delight is lost. We fall victim to our choices.

When United Methodist Bishop Nkulu Ntanda Ntambo from the Republic of Congo visited Dallas, he and his wife stayed with us. He told about eating at a restaurant on his first visit to this country. The server came to take his drink order, offering him many options.

"Coffee, tea?" she inquired. "With milk, sugar, sweetener? Or Coke, Dr. Pepper, Pepsi, Sprite? Regular, diet, caffeine free?"

Finding all these choices confusing, he said simply, "Milk."

"Whole, two percent, or skim?" she asked.

We have so many choices! Not only about what to buy but also about how to live and whether to make joy a companion or a stranger.

Duty and delight are seldom roommates. Duty knows stoicism; delight knows celebration. Duty makes the easy appear difficult; delight makes even the difficult appear easy. In *Angela's Ashes* by Frank McCourt, Aunt Aggie doesn't want to accept the duty of feeding and caring for her nephews while her sister Angela is ill. Grandma says to her, "'Tis a good thing you didn't own that stable in Bethlehem or the Holy Family would still be wanderin' the world crumblin' with the hunger."[17] We let duty steal the joy from our gifts of self.

Many of us find receiving far more difficult than giving. Nouwen tells us that "receiving is an art."[18] We give gifts because we care about others and want to show our gratefulness for them. Receiving a gift provides an opportunity to show our gratitude not only for the gift but, more importantly, for the giver.

Gratefulness includes both giving and receiving. On a snowy winter day, I visited Alexander Nevski Lavra, a beautiful orthodox cathedral in St. Petersburg, Russia. Heavy incense hung in the air. Silent *babushki* crowded the pewless sanctuary. All these elderly women looked alike: drab, worn coats; knitted wool scarves around their necks; dark, knitted caps covering their hair. They were stooped, heads down, unsmiling. One woman brushed against me. She clutched a cane in one hand, an old plastic tote bag in the other. Her right boot was split, and snow layered her foot. She put the widow's mite in the offering bowl and limped toward the altar railing to stand in line for holy bread. As she lifted her eyes toward the priest, they shone with joy from the giving of her gift and from the gift of the Eucharist she was about to receive.

In one of his sermons John Wesley asked, "Does your heart glow with gratitude to the Giver of every good and perfect gift?"[19] Our Creator is Giver. Every morning all of us receive an amazing gift. It is an ancient and daily miracle. With the rising sun, God says to each of us, "Good morning, my child." At day's end—whether we have sailed through calm waters or slogged through quicksand—God speaks again with the setting sun, "I love you, my child."

And we respond....

Rediscovering Hospitality
Scripture: Philippians 1:3-11

Another sign of the season is the innkeeper, who points to rekindling the sacred through hospitality. Mary and Joseph came as strangers from the north, common folk with no wealth, no name to drop, no membership in a hotel Honors Club. These strangers came to the inn (*katalyma*: a room for a guest or for dining), and the innkeeper turned them away because he had no place for them. No one in the crowded inn offered to make a place for them, giving up a bed for this pregnant woman.

Of course, had we been the innkeeper facing weary Mary and Joseph on that holy night, we would have offered the VIP suite, not the stable. Or had we been guests there, we would have given them our room if necessary and gladly slept in the street. We would not have turned the Holy Family away!

But we do. Our lives are already filled with more prominent and demanding lodgers.

Las Posadas ("The Inns"), a tradition that goes back to the Middle Ages and miracle plays, reenacts the innkeeper's lack of hospitality. In Santa Fe, New Mexico, people from the community join together on the Sunday night before Christmas for *Las Posadas*—singing Spanish lyrics adapted from the Gospel of Luke, bringing candles, and following costumed Mary and Joseph around the Plaza as they look for an inn where they can stay. At each inn a devil dressed in red greets the couple and sings that he will not let them have a room in the inn. The crowd boos, and the procession moves on, going from inn to inn as the two are turned away. There was no room for those strangers on that night so long ago—nor is there room for them now.

True hospitality happens when, like the Philippians with Paul, we hold the other in our heart. This kind of hospitality is a beautiful gesture of love. One day as soon as I arrived at her house, my granddaughter Sarah invited me into her room for a pretend tea party. She had it all planned. And we enjoyed it immensely! Imaginary cookies filled our little pink plates, and our small cups overflowed with love.

Hospitality has had a special meaning throughout church history. To this day the Benedictines welcome a guest as they would welcome the Christ. Recently I visited St. Mary's Abbey in West Malling, Kent, England. St. Mary's was begun over nine hundred years ago and is an active Anglican Benedictine convent today. Upon my arrival I was greeted with a kiss on each cheek. I shared in vespers, had tea, and walked in the cloister where centuries of prayers whisper in the silence and bring a sense of peace to harried souls who enter there.

Hospitality that rekindles the sacred is like that offered at St. Mary's Abbey, for each face unveils the face of Christ and each guest is held in the heart. That is our aim on this Advent adventure even though we know that we will fall short. We are imperfect human beings who walk with other imperfect human beings. But that needn't keep us from trying. In Wendell Berry's story "Pray Without Ceasing," Andy's grandmother touches his hand. "If God loves the ones we can't," she said, "then finally maybe we can."[20] Finally maybe we can.

✤

Rediscovering hospitality calls us toward broadening its boundaries. Brother David examined the treatment of strangers in archaic societies and said they were "strangers" in that they were outsiders, unfamiliar, "not belonging to the family."[21] We suspect strangers and fear they may threaten our person, possessions, position, or principles. Even if we find them harmless, we raise an eyebrow if they don't meet our expectations; and we take it upon ourselves to remold them in our likeness instead of welcoming diversity and offering them full acceptance and grace as they are. The Hebrew Scriptures admonish us: "You shall not oppress a stranger, for you know the heart of a stranger, because you were strangers in the land of Egypt" (Exod. 23:9, NKJV). Each of us has had some land-of-Egypt and no-room-in-the-inn experiences.

This is a season to offer hospitality to a stranger—or to one who doesn't share our point of view, especially on a heated issue. Or to one who doesn't meet our expectations—perhaps a colleague, son or daughter, employee or employer, pastor or layperson. Each of these faces masks the face of Christ. When we welcome a stranger to our table, we transform this stranger into a guest. This one, once *estranged*, now sits at the place of honor. We bow together for grace, lift the cup to each other, and pass the bread. How can we ever again view the other in the same way?

✛

Rediscovering hospitality also calls us toward heightening our awareness of how we withhold it. We know that God speaks many languages. All around the globe, people hear God speak in words through the scriptures, readings, and persons. Likewise we hear God speak beyond words—through silence, nature, and the quiet, loving gestures of others. Dietrich Bonhoeffer says, "Our relationship with God must be practised, otherwise we shall not find the right note, the right word, the right language when [God] comes upon us unawares."[22]

We possess many languages to welcome others, languages beyond words, and we withhold hospitality without even being aware of it by remaining monolingual. Georgia O'Keeffe speaks through her paintings, and her book *Georgia O'Keeffe* begins, "The meaning of a word—to me—is not as exact as the meaning of a color."[23] Ways of welcome come in many colors and shades of meaning that we can learn, thereby becoming "multilingual" in order to offer hospitality in a way the other can understand—regardless of background, life experience, and culture. It is not from our own prolific pomp and verbiage that we learn how to speak languages beyond words. It is from presence, from being with others different from ourselves—truly being with them and seeing them with our souls and hearing them with our hearts.

On the wall of my writing nook hangs a piece of wood edged with a border of Xs. It speaks the scriptural language of God:

For God so

loved the

world that
he gave his
one and only
Son.
John 3:16

That piece of wood has no financial value, but in the event of a fire I would save it. My Czech friend made it. He has many excuses to withhold hospitality, to limit its boundaries, and to keep it at a shallow level. He would be justified in sitting in the background and waiting to receive hospitality rather than offering it. He belongs to a unique United Methodist congregation outside of Prague in the Czech Republic, a community in which the members are physically challenged. My friend, like his pastor, lives his life in a wheelchair. His legs cannot function, and his bent and misshapen hands appear useless. But for three months those hands toiled ever so patiently, millimeter by millimeter, to make this beautiful gift. I glance at it on the wall, and through it he continues to teach me that hospitality requires effort and patience and speaking a language the other can understand, for he formed those words not in his native language but in mine.

✦

Rediscovering hospitality also calls us toward deepening its meaning. At its deepest level, hospitality becomes an element of reconciliation, for hospitality and hatred cannot room together. In a homily on reconciliation at the Lambeth Conference, Rev. Canon Susan Cole-King told the story of her father, Leonard Wilson, the Anglican bishop of Singapore. In 1943, he was accused of being a spy and tortured by the *Kempei-tai*, the Japanese military police. On one day of torture seven men with cruel faces took turns flogging him. Enjoying themselves, they asked why he didn't curse them. He replied that he was a follower of Jesus who taught us to love one another.

Leonard Wilson could not protect himself from torture; but he did protect himself from hatred by praying and picturing his torturers as children, for it is hard to hate little children. Through his prayer, a helpful communion hymn came to mind, and at that instant he received a vision of his brutal captors, not as they were, but as they could become if transformed by the love of Christ.

One of the few who survived the torture and hunger, Bishop Wilson returned to Singapore after the war. One day some prisoners were allowed to come from the prison to the cathedral for baptism. Bishop Wilson recognized one of the men standing among them as one who had tortured him, now a prisoner himself. The bishop saw that the power of Christ had transformed the man's face from cruelty into a gentle and peaceful countenance. Rev. Canon Cole-King said her father "had the great joy of confirming one of his torturers." He was able to welcome this man into his heart—this man who had brutally tortured him—as he would have welcomed the Christ.

✦

Paul prays that "your love may overflow more and more with knowledge and full insight" (Phil. 1:9). We do not have to stand with the innkeeper who folds his arms and blocks the door. Advent invites us to reclaim hospitality, to stand with the grown Christ whose arms are extended in love and whose face smiles in welcome.

Reflecting the Light

Scripture: Isaiah 40:1-11

The words of Zechariah to baby John are a sign of Advent. Workers, while removing a partition in the Chapel of St. Gabriel in Canterbury Cathedral, discovered a wall painting of Zechariah, Elizabeth, and the baby. Dating from the 1100s, the painting in faded reds and blues portrays people gathered around the bed where Elizabeth is holding the baby, and Zechariah is writing that the boy is to be named John. The mesmerizing painting invites us into the mood of the moment—the moment that precedes Zechariah's prophecy.

Zechariah has been unable to speak because of his original doubts about the promised birth to occur so late in his and Elizabeth's lives. Luke narrates, "But now, because you did not believe my words, which will be fulfilled in their time, you will become mute, unable to speak, until the day these things occur" (Luke 1:20). Then Luke tells us that upon writing the baby's name, Zechariah's "mouth was opened" (1:64), and he begins to praise God. "Filled with the Holy Spirit"

(1:67) Zechariah speaks his prophecy, which gives us insight on our journey toward rekindling the sacred, a journey toward the Light.

Zechariah says, "By the tender mercy of our God, the dawn from on high will break upon us, to give light to those who sit in darkness and in the shadow of death" (Luke 1:78-79). Georgia O'Keeffe recalls her first memory as "the brightness of light—light all around."[24] I enjoy watching the changing light play with the landscape. With the sun at the horizon, the tiniest shrub casts a long shadow. Centered overhead, there is no shadow at all. The first tree the sun hits begins to shadow the next, which in turn shadows the next, and so on through the row. The biggest tree blocks light from the smaller ones, until gradually the sun moves on across the sky. Though the objects in the landscape remain the same, the changing light and shadows repaint it throughout the day. C. S. Lewis suggests,

> Any patch of sunlight in a wood will show you something about the sun that you could never get from reading books on astronomy. These pure and spontaneous pleasures are 'patches of Godlight' in the woods of our experience.[25]

The changing light serves as a metaphor for our own spiritual struggle. The scenes of our life look different when the light is at the edge of our lives, coming at us from the horizon instead of shining high-noon and centered. We know that sometimes we cast our shadow on another. We also know that there is a side of ourselves we seldom discuss—the shadow side.

Zechariah speaks of being saved from our enemies (Luke 1:71, 74), and so often these enemies reside within us. Each of us has a shadow side. It can sneak up on us and suddenly gain control, influencing our perceptions and feelings, shaping our attitudes and actions, spawning overreaction to situations and fear of whole groups of people. The shadow side gives reign to whatever ancient demons tend to prey on us: gluttony, greed, restless boredom (apathy), depression, anger, vainglory (vanity), lust, and pride. Sometimes we harm ourselves; sometimes we loose our shadow side on another. Instead of dealing with our shadow side, we often pretend it doesn't exist. If we talk about it at all, we discuss it theoretically, safely distanced from personal examples.

My spiritual director has taught me to look at the shadow side without fear. As we learn to recognize its voice, to pull it out into the light, and to examine it, we disarm its power. Therefore, I risk the exposure of a personal experience.

My shadow side ventured forth late at night after the first session of a retreat I was leading. I had felt good about the session—until a woman accosted me. "You're different from what I expected. It's your voice that bothers me. Your style of presentation. Your cheerfulness. You smile too much." She paused for breath and added, "You're not authentic."

Whew! I felt the sting like a slap. My mind tilt-a-whirled. Her words hung juxtaposed to the participants' responsive faces. *Did I misjudge so completely?* She contradicted what I knew about myself: Who I'd been that evening is who I am. Perhaps that's why her comments were so painful.

My shadow side did not surface at that moment. Instead, a spiritual stillness rose within me, a gift for which I will always be grateful. Otherwise, my response could have increased the damage rather than grounding it. I simply said, "I'm sorry you were disappointed."

Later that night when alone, I sat unmoving in a chair, struggling to discern how seriously to take this criticism. To take it too seriously could allow it to reshape me into a negative, frowning presence—and that would indeed be inauthentic. But if I did not take it seriously at all, I might miss an opportunity to grow. Still struggling, I went to bed and turned off the lamp. Tears dampened my pillow.

Then my shadow side came out to coax me. First, vanity: *Who else feels as she does? How can I face them tomorrow? How could I fail so miserably? What am I doing here? I don't need this!* I thought of calling a cab and escaping.

Then anger: *Play on guilt—quote some scriptures tomorrow about not judging others! Be a martyr—whimper about being attacked and how bad it feels! Get revenge—seek support from the responsive faces! Divide and polarize!*

Suddenly I realized that my shadow side was throwing a tantrum. The very act of becoming aware of my shadow side and examining it took away its destructive power. My spiritual director's teaching allowed me to disarm my shadow side and complete the retreat the next day, wounded but spared from wounding.

I don't know that I learned anything particularly helpful from the criticism itself. But in the process of reflecting on that painful situation, I gained deeper insight about my shadow side. Chittister tells us, "When we're driven by agitation, consumed by fretting, we become immersed in our own agenda and it is always exaggerated. We get caught up in things that, in the final analysis, simply don't count."[26] The shadow side gives birth to this agitation syndrome.

Zechariah speaks of the child's guiding "our feet into the way of peace" (Luke 1:79). During our Advent adventure, let's dare to look boldly at our shadow side and try, in Isaiah's words, to "make straight in the desert a highway for our God," trusting that "the uneven ground shall become level, and the rough places a plain" (Isa. 40:3, 4). Chittister describes Benedictine spirituality as "a journey through earthen darkness to the dazzling light that already flames in each of us, but in a hidden place left to each of us to find."[27] We journey on, trusting that we will find the Light that blesses us and that we will learn how to reflect it in a way that blesses others and leads to peace.

Revisioning Community
Scripture: Romans 15:4-13

One of the most visible signs of Advent is the Nativity. We can all envision that scene that points, among other things, to the significance of community in rekindling the sacred. We do not see a figure sitting alone on a golden throne, but a baby lying on hay, watched over by Mary and Joseph. All those called to the manger came in plurals: not one shepherd but the "shepherds." Arriving from the East is not the wise man but the wise "men." Even the angel who appears to the shepherds comes flanked by "a multitude of the heavenly host." In the Nativity all have a place and a part together. So it is in the Christian community.

Brother David discusses "the joy of being together with self, with all, with God." He suggests that "'together' is the word that marks the goal of the religious quest."[28] Community has to do with being *together*, but it is not always easy. The flight attendant and pilot on an airplane teach us about "being together." An attendant assists us in boarding, welcomes us, and helps us find our individual place. The pilot has a flight plan but is open to changes as needed. When all have boarded, found seats, and are ready for the journey, we soar together toward our destination. In the Christian community of faith, each of us is a flight attendant. We welcome people into the community, help them discover their individual place within it, and encourage them to contribute their unique gifts. All of us are also copilots. We help prepare the flight plan and remain open to changes as the Spirit leads. For the members of the community to get off the ground and soar together toward a common destination requires that all get aboard, that all feel part of the community and offer unique gifts, and that we all recognize our own special place and the special place of every other person in the community of faith.

As we look at the Nativity, we see community as inclusive. The community that gathered around the manger included folk of different races and religions, beliefs and traditions, stations and vocations. There were the rich and the poor, the weak and the strong, those from nearby and those from far away. Being inclusive is one of the most difficult challenges that communities face. It is often the source of the shadow side's surfacing in congregations just as it does in people.

Some leaders manipulate through fear or guilt, polarize persons or groups, and foment revenge. The Nazi regime and the Bosnian triangle bear witness to this shadow side in the extreme. But we also see it in congregations, church factions, and denominations when a group allows heated issues to become more important than caring for persons with a different point of view. Probably most (all?) of us have participated in this divisiveness in one way or another at one time or another. When we are divisive, we can be sure that the shadow side is at work.

It is not uncommon, unfortunately, for bishops to be picketed. Being equal-opportunity self-expressions, heated issues bring people from both "sides." Two examples occurred recently within three months of each other. I was with bishops and spouses as a group, leaving a worship service when we were heckled by a placard-carrying crowd made up of picketers who see themselves as tolerant of everyone—except "homosexuals." And I was with bishops and spouses as a group, heckled by a placard-carrying crowd made up of picketers who see themselves as tolerant of everyone—except "homophobes." When we *know* our position is "right"—at whichever end of an emotionally heated continuum we stand—we tend to justify our degradation and mistreatment of people who hold a different perspective. We excuse our behavior on the basis of righteous indignation (which may be a disguise for self-righteous indulgence). Perhaps we tell ourselves that we are doing this for the sake of the community. We even delude ourselves that it makes our destructive words and actions honorable! The guise of protecting community values has justified some heinous things. Coached by the dark side, groups wield weapons of words or perhaps even become capable of tossing bombs.

The baby who taught us to love one another is coming. If we are to be together with God and with all, we will need to make some changes—changes born both of recognizing the message of the Nativity for Christian community and of casting the light of the scripture on the shadow side. As we seek to revision community, we hear Paul's prayer for the Romans echoing for us today: "May the God of steadfastness and encouragement grant you to live in harmony with one another, in accordance with Christ Jesus, so that together you may with one voice glorify the God and Father of our Lord Jesus Christ" (Rom. 15:5-6).

✤

The signs of Advent point us toward rekindling the sacred, but the journey doesn't cease at the end of the season. I think of an Irish tradition described by David Whyte:

> Tir-na-n'og, the land of the young, is the journey of a single step. Just through the gap in the edge, just the other side of the bank of mist. But it takes a lifetime to put yourself in the place from where it is *only* that single step.[29]

Rekindling the sacred is a lifelong journey that takes us through the mist, into the gaps and to the edge.

THOUGHTS AND REFLECTIONS

✢ When did you most feel the presence of God this week? When did you least feel the presence of God this week?

✢ Think about holiness. What does it mean to you? How do you experience it in your life?

✢ Reflect on your baptism. What did it mean to you then? What does it mean to you now?

✢ Reflect on your concept of God in relation to Cardinal Hume's story. What early memory has influenced your image? Consider one of your habitual responses. In what ways does it reveal your attitude toward God?

✢ List (mentally or on paper) the nonmaterial things for which you are grateful. Perhaps you would like to begin and end each day by praising God and expressing your gratitude (with undivided attention).

✢ Ignorant of their future fame—which might have made a difference in his reception—the innkeeper turned the Holy Family away from the inn. What does hospitality mean to you? Where do you set its boundaries? In what ways have you withheld hospitality or experienced hospitality withheld from you? How do you turn away the Christ today?

✢ Evagrius catalogued the passions (habits of the heart in need of healing) as gluttony, greed, lust, depression, anger, restless boredom, vanity, and pride. Which of these passions live in your shadow side? How does bringing them out into the light promote healing?

✢ Does your community of faith reflect the inclusiveness of the Nativity? If not, what are some reasons? How does the shadow side affect your faith community?

Remembering the Song

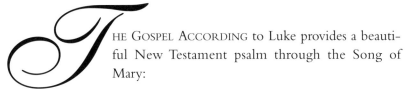

THE GOSPEL ACCORDING to Luke provides a beautiful New Testament psalm through the Song of Mary:

My soul magnifies the Lord,
   and my spirit rejoices in God my Savior,
for he has looked with favor on the lowliness of his servant.
   Surely, from now on all generations will call me blessed;
for the Mighty One has done great things for me,
   and holy is his name.
His mercy is for those who fear him
   from generation to generation.
He has shown strength with his arm;
   he has scattered the proud in the thoughts of their hearts.
He has brought down the powerful from their thrones,
   and lifted up the lowly;
he has filled the hungry with good things,
   and sent the rich away empty.
He has helped his servant Israel,
   in remembrance of his mercy,
according to the promise he made to our ancestors,
   to Abraham and to his descendants forever.
—Luke 1:46-55

In her song Mary "magnifies" (declares the greatness of) the Lord, rejoices in God, and notes her own servanthood—then she proclaims hope for all people. We can read her song as an acknowledgment of God's mighty deeds in the past, and we also can read it as an anticipation of the great deeds to come through the One to be born. We can hear Mary's rejoicing for herself and also for what this One will do for the world.

The *Magnificat* contains a series of allusions to the Hebrew Scriptures and is notably similar to the Canticle of Hannah (1 Sam. 2:1-10). Yet Mary's words do not serve merely as a remembrance from the distant past. They express strong conviction and deep emotion. Mary's song has timeless implications for the song each of our lives sings today. How are we rejoicing in God *now*? *This* season, *this* week, what are we doing to make life better for those we have the power to touch? To make life better than it was last season? Better than it was last week? When the Christ child is born anew in our hearts, his words and works will come alive to us once again; urgency will replace our procrastination; and our good deeds will accompany our goodwill.

Rejoicing in God

Scripture: 1 Thessalonians 5:16-24

> We rejoice in you, O God,
>> for the heavens and the earth
>> for the heavens stretched out like a tent
>> for the earth and all that lives on it
>>> the seas and all that lives in them.
> For the wind that sweeps over the waters
>> the wings of the wind on which you ride
> for the breath of life
>> the Spirit you breathe into us, your creatures.
>>> We praise you, O God, for your good creation.
>
> We rejoice in you, O God,
>> for flame and fire
>>> the sun that rules by day
>>> and the moon that rules by night.

For sunrise and shadows
    North Star and solstice
    the signs and the seasons.
For the light that lights the darkness
    the Light brought by the Child in the manger.
      We praise you, O God, for your good creation.

We rejoice in you, O God,
    for the thunder that brings rain
    for the waters that rise in the mountains
      the springs gushing forth in the valleys
      the streams flowing between the hills
    for the covenant that you will hold up your hand
      and lift the rainbow into the clouds.
For the water quenching the thirst of our souls
    the water of baptism in the name of the Babe.
      We praise you, O God, for your good creation.

We rejoice in you, O God,
    for the seeds and the plants
      and fruit trees of every kind
    for your opening your hand
      and filling us with good things.
For firs reaching toward the heavens
    and tumbleweeds dancing with the earth
for ancient fig trees and the quick-sprouting radish
for rosebush and dandelion
    honeysuckle and purple columbine.
For rich soil and toil in the vineyard
    the wheat that grows supplying bread
for the Eucharist given by the Bread of Bethlehem.
      We praise you, O God, for your good creation.

We rejoice in you, O God,
    for the fish that swarm the seas
      and the birds that fly through the sky
    for whippoorwill and hummingbird
      parrot and flamingo
for the eagle in the spruce and the dove in the cedar
for the butterfly dipping toward the lily.

For cattle and creeping things
    and wild animals of every kind
for the zebra striped white on black or black on white
    the long-necked giraffe and perplexing platypus
for the turtle drawing into its shell
    the sunset and night crawlers and hooting owl.
The earth is full of your creatures,
    living things both small and great.
All is yours
    and you speak your Word of Love
    through the Christmas crib.
        We praise you, O God, for your good creation.

We rejoice in you, O God,
    for humankind,
        created in your image,
        male and female alike.
For love and life
for each of us being one alone
    and all of us one in you.
For the Spirit that abides with us
    through the One born in the stable.
        We praise you, O God, for your good creation.

We rejoice in you, O God,
    for the Sabbath
    the day of blessing
    the sacred day of rest.

We rejoice always in you, O God,
    praying with our lips and our lives
    giving thanks to you
    in moments of laughter and times of tears.

We rejoice always in you, O God,
    not quenching the Spirit
    but hearing the words of the prophets
    and holding fast to what is good,
    abstaining from evil.
We rejoice always in you, O God,
    for you empower us toward peace

and toward keeping our spirit and soul and body
    sound and blameless.
We rejoice in you, O God,
    ever-living, ever-loving Holy One
    beyond all that we can know or imagine
    yet within hearing of our cries and our praise.
    You are our Creator, Redeemer, Sustainer
    you are our Hope
    the Source of Light and Water,
    Eucharist and Word.

We will rejoice in you, O God, as long as we live.
We will sing praise to you, while we have being.
We will meditate and pray and seek to please you.
We will rejoice in you in our souls.
We will praise you, O God!

From Generation to Generation
Scripture: Isaiah 35

One of the Christmas season traditions in southern Louisiana involves building huge bonfires along the levee of the Mississippi River. The stars smile down on the bright blazes that dot the water's winding path. Smoke rises toward the crescent moon, and the dark waves of the river ripple with the light of the flames and clap in celebration. The scent of scorching wood and the musty stench of the Big Muddy stir together in the breeze. Wood crackles in the air's heavy dampness, and cheeks flush from the heat of the fire. Children laugh, and stories abound in Cajun French. The course of the river is marked from bonfire to bonfire, as the course of a people is marked from generation to generation.

Among my treasures are some very old pictures that depict five generations. They begin with my mother and go back in time to her mother and her mother and so on, to my great-great-great-grandparents. My favorite picture is that of my great-grandmother, Mary Smethers. Our guest room hosts her oak bedroom furniture. Through her lingering touch on that old furniture, I know her better now than I did as a child. Sadly, I only remember visiting her once. Just once!

Not knowing her, I piece together her story through anecdotes handed down. Generation to generation.

Born during the Civil War, Grandmother Smethers died in her nineties. She lived simply in a small house in Eureka, Kansas, left alone to rear her children without financial assistance. To her death she remained resolutely independent from those who would help her but fiercely protective of those she could help. Refusing to go on city water when the opportunity came, she kept her own water well; and as long as she lived, she stubbornly climbed down into it herself to clean it. She had no telephone, radio, or TV. She kept up with the news through the local paper, which meant she saw, rather than heard, the names of public officials and sometimes mispronounced them. But it didn't matter; she knew their stories.

In olden days she used to place her bed at an angle away from the wall where, having no closet, she could hang her clothes on hooks screwed into the back of the high headboard and also have some privacy behind it for dressing. The dry sink still holds her blue and white pitcher, separated now from its matching washbowl, broken during our last move. The dresser has a mirror, and when I look into it I think of her standing before it, brushing her long white hair and twisting it into a bun. The old pictures stand on that dresser: my great-grandmother sitting at a treadle sewing machine and her mother at a spinning wheel. My great-great-grandmother spun; my great-grandmother sewed; and my grandmother crocheted lacy sets of booties, caps, and sweaters for new babies born into the family. My mother has crocheted afghans for each of her grandchildren. Generation to generation.

I am blessed to have Grandmother Smethers's Bible, small and black, the binding taped together. She has written in her own hand first names of people and related significant dates—people unknown to me, except for their place of honor in her Bible. From the underlined passages, I learn a bit of her spiritual story. A fitting verse, since she stood among the strong women of her day, is, "Say to those who are of a fearful heart, 'Be strong, do not fear! Here is your God'" (Isa. 35:4). Our God is here for all of us. From generation to generation.

Oftentimes around the Christmas dinner table, we share the family stories, important stories. Nouwen reminds us,

As we grow older we forget many things, but we mostly remember the Thanksgiving or Christmas dinners in our families. We remember them with joy and gratitude or with sadness and anger. They remind us of the peace that existed in our homes or the conflicts that never seemed to get resolved. These special moments around the table stand out as vivid reminders of the quality of our lives together.[1]

The memories, like the levee bonfires, are relit from generation to generation.

Our travels into past generations can be a venture toward fact or toward truth. The intellect does the genealogy, getting the names and dates. But the heart looks for and listens to the stories. We learn the statistics about our ancestors through the facts, but we know them through the stories. Like an organist who plays all the right notes but misses the spirit of the music, we can get all the family data correct and miss the essence. Generation to generation.

Our Advent adventure includes traveling back in time to the beginning of the New Testament and on back to the prophecies of the Hebrew Scriptures. This venture may primarily seek fact or truth. Narrators, in their zeal to make known the truth, can confuse the facts. Our heads examine the data—and sometimes find it contradictory. Our hearts must listen to the stories. We could say that Matthew (1:1-17) gives us the genealogy, and Luke (1:26–2:20) gives us the story. We gain facts about the saints through the data, but we know them through the stories. Facts are passive; they teach us of history and inform our minds. Stories are active; they teach us of faith and transform our souls. Like the organist concentrating on the notes, we too can focus so intently on the facts of the journey that we miss the essence, the Spirit.

Airports offer scenes of reuniting generations. A few weeks before Christmas, I watched people disembark from the plane I was to board. I saw expectant eyes and sudden, big smiles. Wonderful greetings of love abounded. Hugs, close and strong, were given and received—the kind when you really hold on because the other is precious. "You're so tall!" exclaimed a grandmother to her granddaughter, whom she obviously had not seen for a long time. A frail, elderly woman was greeted by her muscular son. Looking up at him tenderly, she asked as she might have when he was a child, "How are you, Sweetie?" A man got off the plane with a youth, telling him, "If we're lucky, a pretty girl will be here—maybe two." And the pretty girls turned out to be his wife and small daughter. The essence of presence mattered, not the data. The Advent adventure is about knowing the stories, telling *the story*, and doing our best to match our own life story to it.

✤

When life's defining moments come—and they will—we can stand with Isaiah, strong and unafraid, trusting that our God is here with us, blessing us from generation to generation.

Scattering the Proud

Scripture: Isaiah 12:2-6

The Song of Mary says that God "has scattered the proud in the thoughts of their hearts" (Luke 1:51). Other Bible versions of that verse speak of the proud "with all their plans" (TEV) and "the arrogant of heart and mind" (NEB). Pride is one of the eight passions mentioned earlier and named by Evagrius Ponticus, a noted fourth-century theologian who analyzed the human soul. A "passion" perverted vision and destroyed love. Inherent in a passion were attitudes and feelings that demonstrated a heart in need of healing.

Pride comes wrapped in packages of different sizes and colors. We've all seen a child with a big smile, looking down at shiny new shoes and proudly sticking one small foot out to show us. Directly or indirectly we know about pride in family, in a church, in our country, in a job well done. Surely these small prides are permissible—unless they dominate our hearts, consume our plans, give birth to arrogance. Pride stands juxtaposed to humility. Antony the Great, born in the middle of the third century and called "The Father of Monks," said, "I saw all the devil's traps set upon the earth, and I groaned and said: 'Who do you think can pass through them?' And I heard a voice saying: 'Humility.'"[2]

First Peter relates pride to our relationships with others: "And all of you must clothe yourselves with humility in your dealings with one another, for 'God opposes the proud, but gives grace to the humble'" (5:5). The sayings of the desert fathers reflect three dimensions of humility in relationships. The first is forgiveness. Someone asked an old man of the desert, "What is humility?" He answered, "If you forgive a brother who has wronged you before he is penitent towards you."[3] Another father defined humility in this way: "To do good to them that do ill to you,"[4] which is the second dimension.

The third dimension has to do with standing not in judgment, above one who errs—but in compassion, beside that one, sharing the burden. An ancient story tells of two monks in Celia. The younger monk told the older one that he had sinned. "The old man said: 'Are you penitent?' And the brother said: 'Yes.' The old man said: 'I will carry half the burden of the sin with you.'"[5] When we are "arrogant of heart and mind," we find it hard to forgive one who wrongs us and even harder to do good to one who does ill to us. It is perhaps still harder to help carry, day in and day out, the burden of another's shortcomings.

Paul relates pride to faith, saying that we "stand only through faith" and admonishing us: "So do not become proud, but stand in awe" (Rom. 11:20). Abba Mathois warns against creating "a bubble reputation."[6] Whatever term we use for this passion of religious pride—for example, being self-righteous or flaunting piety—it perverts vision and love and indicates a heart in need of healing. Abba Antony once said after testing a brother: "You are like a house with a highly decorated facade, where burglars have stolen all the furniture out of the back door."[7] Facades and flourishes can be lovely to look at, but they are not faith.

In *Angela's Ashes*, we glimpse religious pride through the eyes of a child. Frankie's boyhood friend Fintan Slattery raises his hand in class to answer that he knows who stood at the foot of the cross. Frankie narrates,

> Of course Fintan knows who stood at the foot of the cross. Why wouldn't he? He's always running off to Mass with his mother, who is known for her holiness. She's so holy her husband ran off to Canada to cut down trees, glad to be gone and never to be heard from again....They go to Mass and Communion rain or shine and every Saturday they confess to the Jesuits who are known for their interest in intelligent sins, not the usual sins you hear from people in lanes who are known for getting drunk and sometimes eating meat on Fridays before it goes bad and cursing on top of it....He says he wants to be a saint when he grows up, which is ridiculous because you can't be a saint till you're dead....

Of course he knows who stood at the foot of the cross. He probably knows what they were wearing and what they had for breakfast and now he's telling Dotty O'Neill it was the three Marys.[8]

To seek sainthood contradicts saintliness. Intentional worship attendance is one of the Christian disciplines, but calling attention to it breaks another of the disciplines. True holiness cannot be flaunted, for it stands in awe.

In the Letter of James, as in the First Letter of Peter, we find the words: "God opposes the proud, but gives grace to the humble" (4:6); but in James pride relates to a lack of submission to God. Describing one monk, Abba Antony commented, "I think that monk is like a ship laden with a rich cargo but not yet certain of reaching port in safety."[9] When we submit ourselves to God we do not relinquish our own responsibility; we find ourselves supported by a bold trust as we sail with a scriptural guide for reaching port. Pride can lead us astray, especially in a society drowning in gimmicks. I know a congregation that calls itself "The Church of Success." The name itself rings discordant. *Success* is a prideful word unrelated to the teachings of the Christ, a word not found in any recognized translation of the New Testament.[10] Obedience is about servanthood and sacrifice—but success sells better. A "church of success" may be a ship laden with rich cargo; and all the people sailing on it may be enjoying the voyage, but its guidebook for reaching port—color graphics and all—may be unreliable in the storms. Both individuals and congregations have trouble with obedience. We misuse the faith, a difficulty frequently rooted in our lack of humility. Nouwen suggests,

> We have to keep looking both ways to remain humble *and* confident, humorous *and* serious, playful *and* responsible. Yes, the human being is very small and very tall. It is the tension between the two that keeps us spiritually awake.[11]

Only through spiritual wakefulness can our hearts begin to heal and our pridefulness cease to reign. Our arrogance gives way to gratitude and praise. We seek the Light, not the limelight; and with Isaiah we "give thanks to the Lord" and "proclaim that his name is exalted." We sing "praises to the Lord" and "sing for joy" (Isa. 12:4, 5, 6).

Bringing Down the Powerful
Scripture: Luke 3:7–18

As Mary sings that God "has brought down the powerful from their thrones" (Luke 1:52), we recall that this song celebrates what God has done in the past and anticipates what God will do through the birth of the coming One. We can think of a few leaders in foreign countries that we would like to have brought down—perhaps even some people across town or up the street. But our Advent adventure does not focus on other people's power and bringing them down from their thrones. Our Advent adventure emphasizes the way we use *our* power. And all of us have power to some degree.

It isn't that we don't know what to do with power. When the crowds ask John what they should do, he replies, "Whoever has two coats must share with anyone who has none; and whoever has food must do likewise" (Luke 3:11). To the tax collectors he says, "Collect no more than the amount prescribed for you" (Luke 3:13). And to the soldiers he states, "Do not extort money from anyone by threats or false accusation, and be satisfied with your wages" (Luke 3:14). We've known what to do with power for two millennia: Share. Don't cheat. Don't extort, threaten, or lie; and don't be greedy. We can go back even further, for Micah put it this way: "O mortal,…what does the Lord require of you but to do justice, and to love kindness, and to walk humbly with your God?" (6:8).

Whether we live in a penthouse or a prison, however near to home we stay or far the range of our lives, whatever our situation, all of us have the power to be present in the moment and to bless those lives that intersect ours. This blessing, of course, is not a matter of going about saying, "Bless you, my child." It is about encountering the other, showing through our actions that the other *counts* to us. We bless the other by valuing him or her. In *Beach Music* by Pat Conroy, Jack speaks of his mother, Lucy, following her death:

> I learned that week that my mother possessed a small genius for the right gesture. She had done thousands of things she did not have to do only because they felt comfortable to her. She had been prodigal with unnoticed, artless moments of making people happy to be alive.[12]

Lucy demonstrated the power of presence in the moment, which can become the power to bless. This is no small power! But we often squander it.

The babe who became the Christ offers many gifts. One is a new perspective of power: If we hold a position of power (for example, in the government or work force or church or family or through our influence on others), we are not to exercise our power from a "throne," sitting above others and authoritatively controlling them (or operating under the table, manipulating them). We are not to use people to accumulate more power for ourselves. No! Instead, we are to step away from the throne (or out from under the table) and walk with others, respecting them, honoring them, and using our power to empower them. The faithful purpose of power is not self-aggrandizement; the faithful purpose is to bless.

Power sought and used for blessing would transform our world. We think of the Balkans and parts of Africa and the school war zones of our own gun-toting children. The use of power for the sake of empowerment would change leaders and peoples in nations and neighborhoods, thus fulfilling Isaiah's prophecy: "Violence shall no more be heard in your land, devastation or destruction within your borders; you shall call your walls Salvation and your gates Praise" (Isa. 60:18).

In an article in *Time* entitled "Our Century...And the Next One," Walter Isaacson states that America's "idealist streak is a source of its global influence." He suggests that the country's influence stems not just from its "military might but from the power and appeal of its values." He concludes his article: "The ultimate goal of democracy and freedom, after all, is not to pursue material abundance but to nurture the dignity and values of each individual."[13] Pursuing material abundance is about power; nurturing individual dignity and values is about empowerment and blessing.

As each of us is born into a specific culture and age, so was Jesus. At his birth, Augustus ("august, exalted, revered"; originally named Gaius Octavius) ruled as emperor of the Roman Empire. His defeat of Antony and Cleopatra in Egypt completed possession of the vast lands surrounding the Mediterranean Sea, including Judea. The Romans saw themselves as the rulers of the civilized world. After Rome's long political and military turmoil, Augustus ushered in a new age of peace. He developed an efficient postal system. He improved the harbors and built bridges, aqueducts, and roads that connected Rome to the major cities of the empire. He constructed beautiful buildings—some still standing—and boasted that he "found Rome brick and left it marble." Despite all the contributions of Augustus Caesar, the first emperor of the vast Roman Empire, all that most of us today know about him is that he figures in the historical background of a babe born in a stable.

Augustus clutched power; Jesus empowered. Augustus controlled; Jesus blessed. Augustus enforced the power of law; Jesus exhibited the power of love. Morton Kelsey sums it up this way, "Augustus and Jesus: the world and the Spirit."[14]

When we reflect honestly and deeply on the way we use our own power, do we find ourselves closer in style to Augustus or to Jesus? to the way of the world or the way of the Spirit?

Lifting Up the Lowly
Scripture: Isaiah 61:1-4, 8-11

The *Magnificat* reminds us to lift up the lowly (Luke 1:52). Abba Poeman told about a brother who asked Abba Alonius: "'What is lowliness?' And the old man said: 'To be lower than brute beasts; and to know that they are not condemned.'"[15] All of God's creatures have worth. The angel's appearance to the shepherds, viewed as the lowest strata of Jewish society, signals the universality of God's loving grace. Like members of a global bell choir, each of us is created as something beautiful; each is necessary and of equal importance in rendering the sacred song. But some notes remain silent. Isaiah says that God

> has sent me to bring good news
>   to the oppressed,
> to bind up the brokenhearted,
> to proclaim liberty to the captives,
>   and release to the prisoners;...
> to comfort all who mourn
>   —Isaiah 61:1-2

Are these the ones about whom Mary sings?

Being a school counselor was my ministry in the workplace as a layperson when Bill and I lived in Oklahoma. During that time those of whom Isaiah speaks touched my life as never before. Among the faces that scroll through my memory are a pregnant eighth grader, a seventh-grade girl who attempted suicide, and a boy who brought a gun to school. And Peter. And Stevie.

Peter, a fifth grader, was a quiet, sensitive boy. His teachers expressed their concern about his falling asleep in class. When I talked with him, he told me that he was responsible for his four younger brothers and sisters at night. He worried that something would happen to them, so he always tried to stay awake until morning.

Our impulse is to pass judgment on his mother—until we hear more of the story. When I visited with her, I learned that she had been in a terrible marriage. Her husband physically abused her and the children. It had taken her a long time to gather the courage to leave the situation; she didn't know how she could take care of her children and also earn a living. But one night her husband hurt her so badly she feared he might kill her if she did not get out of the marriage. "And then," she asked, her eyes distant, "what would happen to my children?"

The woman had taken a night job so she could be home in time to get her children up, fix them breakfast, and get them off in the mornings. She slept during the day and was there for them when they got home from school. She supervised their homework, fixed dinner, and then went to her minimum-wage job while they slept. She had no family nearby, no one to help. She was doing what she felt was *least harmful* for her children.

There are too many Peters and their mothers in the world for us to take on the entire cause. But how do we lift up the ones in our immediate community?

❖

Stevie often sat beside me at the round table in my office. This arrangement gave his kindergarten teacher the needed escape valve to handle him while remaining sane. He was a thin, blond-haired, blue-eyed little boy whose front teeth were missing and, most of the time, so were his glasses. He got into more mischief than any other student. He could grab the fastest, laugh the loudest, move the quickest, and wiggle the most of any kindergartner in the history of that school. He was always in trouble—and probably always will be.

Stevie had never seen his father. His mother's drug use before his birth left him affected by attention-deficit hyperactivity disorder (a disorder that has a variety of origins). A couple of years before Stevie's birth, his mother had left her oldest daughter, five at the time, home alone with a baby sister. The baby drowned in the bathtub while the mother was gone. Stevie's big sister came to my office frequently, once showing me a photo she carried around with her—a picture of that baby in a coffin. The fourth baby was born drug dependent and so severely damaged mentally and physically that the infant was unable to leave the hospital and died at the age of three months.

There are too many Stevies in the world for us to take on the entire cause. But how do we lift up the ones in our immediate community?

✥

After our move to Louisiana, I became part of a Kairos team, a faith-based ministry similar to Cursillo or The Walk to Emmaus designed especially for prisons. A Kairos team spends Thursday evening through Sunday evening working with a group of prison residents who are self-selected and also approved by prison officials. My team worked with the state women's prison.

Sondra, one of the friends I made in that institution, is a beautiful woman in her late thirties. Her striking dark eyes are sensitive and soul deep rather than hardened. Like all the participants in Kairos, she takes responsibility for her crime. A teenaged mother, she was imprisoned when her two children were preschoolers; they have recently reached their twenties. Their grandmother in another state reared them. In all these years, Sondra has never seen them. Her eyes cloud as she speaks of her children, the same love surfacing in her face and her voice that all parents know. Her only dream is to see them again someday.

There are too many Sondras in the world for us to take on the entire cause. But how do we lift up the ones in our immediate community?

✥

How do we lift up the "lowly"? Who among us feels called within our own community to bring the good news of intervention and healing to children oppressed in so many ways by drugs?

Who among us feels called within our own community to bind up the brokenhearted single parents whose choices for their children cannot be made from a wide array of good and best but are limited between most harmful and least harmful?

Who among us feels called within our own community to proclaim liberty to the children held captive by our judicial system? Many fine judges agonize over their decisions. But in too many situations the primary concern becomes expediting case removals from a crowded social services docket; putting children's blood ahead of their benefit handles a case more quickly. How do we justify leaving children in (or returning them to) destructive environments rather than facilitating adoption to parents who would provide a loving, nurturing, and stable relationship?

Who among us feels called within our own community to assist families in order to improve the circumstances of babies limited by conditions of birth—those born imprisoned by prenatal drug addiction or born into hunger or hopeless economic conditions?

Who among us feels called within our own community to comfort those who mourn the loss—through death or separation—of the ones they cherish the most?

Who among us feels called to lift up the lowly in some other way? Suppose that all of us removed the scales from our eyes and each year tried to lift even one of the "lowly," touching that single life in a way that gives hope, recognition of worth, and the practical assistance necessary to ring the first note in our sacred song. If each of us did that, think of the potential for changed lives in a decade or a score, a quarter or half a century. Think of the number of folk who might be lifted up by the end of our own lifespan, playing their unsilenced notes.

Who among us feels content to do nothing? Nouwen says, "A traitor, according to the literal meaning of the Greek word for 'betraying,' is someone who hands the other over to suffering."[16] When we have a way to lift up one of the "lowly" and do not, do we hand that child of God over to continued suffering and, thereby, betray Christ? Betrayal, of course, is not new. In the early centuries of the church one of the desert fathers observed that once "charity ruled, and each one drew [the] neighbour upward. Now charity is growing cold, and each of us draws [the] neighbour downward."[17] God's love encompasses us even in our betrayal. Nevertheless, we make the choice.

In *Beach Music*, Ruth Fox tells her story as a young Jewish girl during World War II when the Nazis invaded Poland. She was saved by being hidden and eventually arrived in the United States. She speaks of getting off the ship in South Carolina: "Hundreds of strangers are here to greet me....They, who do not know me, embrace me. They, who are not kin to me, raise me up as their daughter. They, who owe me nothing, give me back my life."[18]

Lifting up the lowly is about greeting the stranger, embracing one unknown, treating as family those who are not kin—lifting toward life those to whom we owe nothing.

Filling the Hungry

Scripture: Zephaniah 3:14-20

Mary sings of filling the hungry with good things (Luke 1:53). Primary to our well-being is filling the hunger for food. We also know a deep hunger for the Spirit.

Many of us have no experience of hunger except through dieting or fasting. We commonly rise from the table saying, "Oh! I ate too much!" It is not possible for me to write experientially about the hungry because the only times I've known hunger were chosen, not imposed by necessity. Once long ago I stood in a soup line, posing as one of the poor and homeless in order to learn how it felt and to see how the servers treated the served, but what I learned was that I couldn't really know how it felt because the next day I would return home to a full pantry, meat in the freezer, and milk in the fridge.

In *Angela's Ashes*, Frank McCourt portrays hunger during his childhood. His mother receives from a charity a "docket for groceries" for Christmas dinner. She hopes for a goose or a ham, but the butcher will give her nothing but a pig's head. Frankie recalls the scene:

> Mam says the pig's head isn't right for Christmas and he says 'tis more than the Holy Family had in that cold stable in Bethlehem

long ago. You wouldn't find them complaining if someone offered them a nice fat pig's head.

No, they wouldn't complain, says Mam, but they'd never eat the pig's head. They were Jewish.[19]

We expect the hungry to be grateful for their little Christmas basket or whatever else we do, but "I'm-so-good" generosity fades when we compare what we give with what we keep.

John Wesley wrote about our acts matching our faith, calling for "all that believe themselves [God's] children, to evidence it by showing mercy to the poor....I would not desire them to lose one meal in a week, but to use as cheap food, clothes, &c., as possible."[20] I can picture Wesley shaking his head at our practices today. Even when we want to shed those pounds from overeating, we spend more money for diet foods and weight loss programs rather than less money for a smaller amount of food. Says Bishop Rueben P. Job, "Wesley believed that when we purchase something unnecessary or extravagant, we...take bread from the hands of the hungry."[21]

This image jolts us. Guilt, however, serves no purpose. What we need is an increased awareness of how far removed we are from the experience of those for whom hunger is a way of life. With Advent comes an engraved invitation to open our eyes to see the hidden ones—especially the little ones—who go to bed (if they have a bed) with their tummies empty instead of filled with good things. At the bottom left-hand corner of this Advent invitation to awareness, we find the letters *RSVP*.

Advent also invites us to open our ears to those who hunger for the Spirit. "The Lord, your God, is in your midst," says Zephaniah. He adds that God "will rejoice over you with gladness" and "renew you in [God's] love" (Zeph. 3:17). When we give bread without the intent of these words, we give only half a gift. If we could create a world in which no child and no adult ever again had to endure hunger, people around the globe would be filled—but still hungry. Bread alone is not enough; we hunger also for the Bread of Life.

I recall seeing a curious piece in an exhibit of musical instruments in the Metropolitan Museum of Art in New York. It was a walking stick that also served as a flute. Perhaps the Christmas season makes us more conscious of the hungry than other times of the year. We give a walking stick to help them through the holidays. That is considerate, but it is a minimal gift. How much better if that walking stick were also the flute of the good news that we and they *together* are among those God will exult over "with loud singing as on a day of festival" (Zeph. 3:17-18).

Sending the Rich
Scripture: Psalm 126

Mary sang of filling the hungry with good things and sending the rich away empty. Her son, when grown, takes this to a deeper level, showing compassion for all: He fills the hungry with good things *without* sending the rich away empty.

We do not need to limit the word *rich* to money. The poorest of the poor can know abundant life from a centered soul, and the richest of the rich can know scarcity of joy, meaning, and purpose. But Mary's Song deals with material wealth. *Rich* is a relative word. Compared to a person who has no bread, a person with sugar is rich. Compared to a billionaire, a millionaire is a thousand times less rich. As a descriptive word, *rich* embarrasses some people, evokes guilt in others and at times is flaunted. In the antebellum homes of the South, families boasted of their wealth by displaying expensive lemons in a silver bowl on the dining table or "puddling" the draperies (letting the panels trail beneath the windows in a puddle of folds on the floor) to show that the family could afford to be superfluous.

In speaking about "The Use of Money," John Wesley says to "gain all you can." But he sets clear limits: This money is not to come "at the expense" of life or our health, nor by hurting our mind or our neighbor. He states that if we love everyone as ourselves, we cannot "devour" anyone's lands and houses, specifically by "gaming," "over-grown bills," and "pawn-broking"; and we cannot sell anything that tends to "impair health." We are to gain all we can "by honest wisdom, and unwearied diligence."[22]

Next, Wesley tells us, "Save all you can." He warns against throwing away "the precious talent" into the sea or in idle expenses or using it "merely" to gratify the desires of the flesh, the eye, or pride. He raises particular concern about wasting it by "enlarging the pleasure of tasting." He says, "I do not mean, avoid gluttony and drunkenness only:

An honest Heathen would condemn these. But there is…an elegant epicurism, which…cannot be maintained without considerable expense. Cut off all this expense!"²³ Many of us blush at this one, especially during Advent!

Perhaps the rich man who comes to Jesus (Mark 10:17-30; Matt. 19:16-29; Luke 18:18-25) also has involved himself in the process of gaining and saving. He runs up to Jesus and kneels before him, asking what he must do to inherit eternal life. He says he has kept the commandments regarding murder, adultery, stealing, false witness, defrauding, and honoring his parents. Jesus listens, then looking at him

> loved him and said, "You lack one thing; go, sell what you own, and give the money to the poor, and you will have treasure in heaven; then come, follow me." When he heard this, he was shocked and went away grieving, for he had many possessions (Mark 10:21-22).

The man was not sent away; he "went away" of his own accord, "grieving."

As do we. The radical expectations of the good news shock us as well, and so we excuse ourselves. As Jesus did not judge the man or scold him or send him away but "loved him," so it is with us. Like the rich man, we feel Jesus' love even as we turn away, and we also grieve.

Back to John Wesley's sermon. Not only does he tell us to gain all we can and save all we can, he also says "give all you can." He suggests that saving is nothing unless we point our savings toward "a farther end": "You may as well throw your money into the sea, as bury it in the earth. And you may as well bury it in the earth, as in your chest, or in the bank of England." Wesley considers ineffective use of money the same as throwing it away.²⁴ The idea of giving probably does not trouble us—but the idea of *generous* giving is another matter!

Jesus spoke to his disciples: "How hard it will be for those who have wealth to enter the kingdom of God!" (Mark 10:23). The disciples did not judge the rich man either or send him away. In fact, Jesus' words "perplexed" them, partially perhaps because Jesus numbered the rich among his friends.

Again Jesus spoke, "Children, how hard it is to enter the kingdom of God!" (Mark 10:24). This time Jesus did not limit the difficulty of entering the kingdom only to the rich. It is hard for all of us—rich and poor alike—to act on the words of our common global prayer: "Thy kingdom come." We cling to lesser goals. We don't follow Jesus' giving way of living.

Jesus continued,

> "It is easier for a camel to go through the eye of a needle than for someone who is rich to enter the kingdom of God." They were greatly astounded and said to one another, "Then who can be saved?" (Mark 10:25-26).

This time the disciples were not merely perplexed by what Jesus said but astounded. As are we. Is this challenge more difficult for us than for something as large as a camel to go through something as small as the eye of a needle? Perhaps our difficulty in following Jesus comes from our acquired fondness for possessions that disallows reducing them; and we can't drag all these material things through the eye of stewardship. Or perhaps we are so accustomed to accumulation that changing the pattern from getting to giving seems insurmountable, and this is a requirement for following Jesus. Or perhaps we tie our identity to our possessions, and stripping them away evokes a fear that this will also peel away our personhood, leaving only bones. This fear of loss is greater than our trust in God.

Jesus looked at the astounded disciples and said, "For mortals it is impossible, but not for God; for God all things are possible" (Mark 10:27). Trust in God cannot be bought or beguiled. We develop this trust through practice of the spiritual disciplines.

We recall a saying in Proverbs: "Whoever trusts in…riches will fall, but the righteous will thrive like a green leaf" (Prov. 11:28, NIV). Riches and thriving do not have to be contradictory. Wesley explains that "the Possessor of heaven and earth" placed each of us "here, not as a proprietor, but a steward," entrusted "for a season, with goods of various kinds; but the sole property of these still rests in [God]." We are God's and are to be employed for God "in such a manner, that it may be all an holy sacrifice, acceptable through Christ Jesus."[25] By trusting God and following Christ, we may use our riches faithfully and become a source of joy through sharing.

The psalmist begins, "When the Lord restored the fortunes of

Zion, we were like those who dream" (Ps. 126:1). The rich have an opportunity to be the hands of God in a special way through access to the resources that can help restore the fortunes of a community and keep alive the dreams of the poor. Just as the powerful are to use their power to empower others, the rich are to use their riches to enrich others.

Perhaps the rich are not sent away—but *sent!*

✦

During a Kwanza celebration at St. Luke's United Methodist Church in Dallas, a man told a story about an African village. The villagers held fast to their tradition that if one of them was in trouble, all the people in the entire village would stop what they were doing and come to help.

One of the men built his new home high on a hill above the village. He could look down and see the long, winding river flowing beside the village. One day while working outside, the man glanced down and noticed that far in the distance the river was rushing faster than usual and wildly overflowing its banks. He knew that when the river reached the village, it would flood and the people would drown.

The man shouted down to the people as loudly as he could, but they couldn't hear him. He didn't have time to go all the way into the village to warn them—they must start for higher ground right away .

He thought quickly and realized he could do only one thing. He could count on the people to follow their tradition—*when one of us is in trouble, we all stop whatever we are doing and go immediately to help.* So the man set fire to his new house.

One of the people looked up, saw the fire, and called the others. Everyone climbed to the top of the hill to help the man whose house was burning, and all the people in the village were saved from drowning in the flood.

The story shows us that if we are unaware of our surroundings, we will miss opportunities to serve. If we do not pay attention to the needs of others, our efforts to help may be ineffective. If we do not bother to learn others' customs and interests, we will not know how to speak love in a second language, a language they will understand. If we are unwilling to sacrifice our possessions for the sake of others, we will remain on the hilltop looking down, watching God's children be swept away.

THOUGHTS AND REFLECTIONS

✣ When did you most feel the presence of God this week? When did you least feel the presence of God this week?

✣ If you were to write a litany rejoicing in God, what would you include?

✣ Think about a family story carried forward from generation to generation. What is its blessing? What is its truth?

✣ When have you experienced "prideful" religion, your own or someone else's?

✣ In what helpful way has another used his or her power for you? How have you used your power for another person or group?

✣ During this Advent adventure, how do you feel called to "lift up the lowly"?

✣ Think about a hunger you have experienced. How is that hunger filled?

✣ Reflect on the section "Sending the Rich." Where do you see yourself? How could you share your riches—of whatever kind—to help transform your small part of the world?

Reclaiming the Star

ISHOP RUEBEN P. JOB says, "To live with God and to walk with Jesus Christ profoundly shapes and transforms the individual life."[1] Reclaiming the star is about shaping and transforming our lives. To live with God sets us on an inner journey—soul time. To walk with Jesus Christ sets us on an outer journey—service time.

Going to Bethlehem
Scripture: Luke 2:1-7

As Christians we begin that journey by going to Bethlehem. The word *Bethlehem* means "house (place) of bread." It was a village in the grainfields. The babe who is born in the "house of bread" becomes the "Bread of Life." Another word is also associated with Bethlehem. An old London hospital for emotionally disturbed persons was named the Hospital of St. Mary of Bethlehem. Because of the noise and confusion in that place, the Middle English word *bedlem* was derived from *Bethlehem*. Our journey to Bethlehem is not all neat and tidy. Life gets messy. More than bread awaits us on our adventure; we also experience bedlam—as did Mary.

Mary is revered throughout Christendom, even viewed by Pope John Paul II as worthy of deification. We can easily forget her human-ness, her joy as a mother who reared her child, watched him grow into manhood, and participated in his ministry—at times through her pres-ence and always through her prayers—and who suffered at his cruci-fixion. But Mary doesn't know about that yet as she travels to Bethlehem.

The Gospel According to Luke tells us that because of a required registration Joseph and Mary, who are expecting a child, go from Naz-areth in Galilee to Bethlehem in Judea. Luke, eager to move on to more important things, leaves it at that—just a one-verse journey. But what of that journey? Surely Mary would not choose such a journey at this time! Let's walk beside her as she goes to Bethlehem.

Pregnant Mary has already said, "Here am I, the servant of the Lord" (Luke 1:38). Now she rides for nearly a hundred miles through this hilly region on a bouncing burro. Quietly she endures backaches and leg cramps, and silently she smiles as she feels life within her, the child kicking beneath her ribs.

Mary and Joseph head southward, viewing the nature of the land, not realizing that its flowers, trees, and birds will one day embellish the parables of the One to come. They make their way through the de-scending slopes toward the historic Plain of Esdraelon (the Valley of Jezreel), which separates Galilee from Samaria and is crossed by caravan routes and traveled by soldiers and merchants.

Mary and Joseph travel precariously on unstable soil, passing through a range of hills composed of eroded limestone, soft and porous. The weather varies from day to day, at times blowing grit against Mary's face and at times drenching her with rain. They know the ever-present fear of bandits. With each crumbling hill, Mary leaves her family farther behind, and each day draws her nearer to the birth of the baby. Perhaps a gnawing fear grows within her about facing the unknown, so alone.

When the couple reach Samaria, the slopes ascend once more, and the peaks of Mount Ebal and Mount Gerizim rise above them. This is the most fearful part of the journey because the Jews are, at best, toler-ated among Samaritans and, at worst, unwelcome. Mary wearies of traveling, of seeing in each face the face of a stranger. Perhaps from time to time she reaches for the assurance of Joseph's hand.

Safely out of Samaria, they begin the descent through the Judean hills. Finally, about six miles south of Jerusalem, they reach Bethlehem. Mary, exhausted and heavy with child, is relieved that they have arrived. Knowing the time is soon, she closes her eyes, resting a moment as Joseph talks with the innkeeper. A smile appears on her face as she visualizes washing off the grime from the journey and lying down in a comfortable place. Then Joseph turns back toward her, shaking his head. There is no room in the inn.

Now we get two verses from Luke: "While they were there, the time came for her to deliver her child. And she gave birth to her first-born son" (Luke 2:6-7). Except for Joseph, Mary is alone. No family. No friends. No familiar women from her community. No grandparents waiting nearby to rejoice and help. No aunts standing in line to get a turn at cuddling the newborn. Perhaps Joseph finds someone among the strangers who is skilled and can help Mary as the birth approaches. But birthing a firstborn is no time to be left with strangers!

Mary has reached Bethlehem, the end of one journey that opens onto the next journey. The birth of the babe creates much ado! (As there is still much ado over that birth today.) Angels and shepherds and the magi who follow the star to Bethlehem. Luke tells us that "as for Mary, she treasured all these things and pondered them in her heart" (Luke 2:19, JB).

While Mary's heart rejoices, the laws of Leviticus classify her as "unclean":

A woman who becomes pregnant and gives birth to a son will be ceremonially unclean for seven days, just as she is unclean during her monthly period....Then the woman must wait thirty-three days to be purified from her bleeding. She must not touch anything sacred or go to the sanctuary until the days of her purification are over (Lev. 12:2, 4, NIV).

Leviticus 12:5 prescribes a different regulation if a daughter is born instead of a son: The time for being "unclean" doubles to two weeks and the "waiting to be purified" also doubles, from thirty-three to sixty-six days. Under the laws of Leviticus, being "unclean" is considered to be a contagious condition. If anyone touches the woman or the bed she lies on or a chair she sits in, "he will be unclean till evening" (Lev. 15:19-23, NIV). We wonder about Joseph. Which was more important to him—the risk of contagion or the compassion of sitting beside Mary on her makeshift bed and tenderly enfolding her hand?

According to Leviticus, through no intentional or accidental wrongdoing of any kind, the Holy Mother cannot enter the sanctuary or touch anything holy. But she holds the babe in her arms, this Son of God, who will later teach his followers to revere the law but not at the expense of compassion—for the greatest commandment is love, love of God and love of all God's children.

We worship Jesus Christ as fully human and fully divine. His birth in the stable attests to God's intention that we see in Jesus our own humanity—a baby vulnerable at birth in the cave and a man vulnerable to death on the cross. We have tried so far during our Advent adventure to put out of our minds awareness that the manger leads to the cross and to envision this time of preparation as Mary and Joseph might have experienced it. Yet we do know about the cross. In our minds we see beyond Mary's holding Jesus in her arms as a baby. This joyful scene is poignant for we know what is ahead, and in our hearts we also see the *Pietà*, Michelangelo's beautiful sculpture of Mary holding Jesus across her lap once again—this time after his crucifixion. His head rests on her shoulder, and her face portrays a mother's deep suffering at the death of her beloved son.

✥

At times we, like Mary, face journeys we would not choose. They intrude into our lives—perhaps a family transition or the loss of a dream or a change in job or health. Or a sudden physical or mental impairment or the death of a loved one. Or perhaps our journey is an inner one that takes us through the darkness of despair and a spiritual void.

The journey is not smooth. The ground is unsure. We face storms along the way. We have hills to climb and descend, valleys to pass through, times of fear and loneliness, of arid soul and overflowing troubles. Some spaces feel foreign to us, and we guard against part of ourselves being stolen away. We grow weary and need assurance. When we think we have come to the end of the journey and can rest at last, we may not find the "inn" we had hoped for or expected. We don't journey through change without changing. It gives birth to a new way of being and doing and living in the world. This change in us ripples into our relationships. We may meet those who whisper "unclean" and keep their distance.

Congregations also face difficult journeys with these same dynamics. The journey required may not be the one of choice, and it may end differently from what was expected. Members may divide as though they fear a contagion, and those on each side of this relational "Continental Divide" shout selected scripture verses to support their point of view. As persons and congregations, we can easily forget that God is with us in all our journeys and that God's love transcends culture-limited and opinion-biased understandings. In the babe, Love is born—a living Love, who taught and demonstrated the greatest commandment.

The Homeless One, fully human and fully divine, teaches us a faith of hope and humility, compassion and courage. To be faithful as an individual or a community is to say with Mary, "Here am I, the servant of the Lord" (Luke 1:38). Our journey to Bethlehem helps us discover the certainty that the end of one journey—inward or outward—will open onto the next journey, even at death.

Glimpsing the Star
Scripture: Matthew 2:1-12

It is hard to glimpse the star from the crowded tollway of our fast-paced lives. Even if we do happen to glimpse the star, we are cautious about following it like the magi. Before we begin, we flip on the weather channel to see if snow is predicted. We check out an astronomy web page so we can E-mail for the star's precise location—we can't just strike out without knowing the exact destination! We request a day-by-day itinerary from the travel agent with reservations confirmed. We want assurance that at the end of each day's journey we'll have a hot shower, a king-size bed with clean sheets, and access to TV.

No wandering along in a slow caravan, swaying on dirty camels, smelling sweat, and tasting dust like the magi—not for us, thank you. They couldn't even catch the ten o'clock news to hear how many gladiators had been killed in Rome that day, to find out if any of the

Empire's governors had been toppled, to see an update on the building progress of the Pantheon, or to get a special report on how Caesar Augustus planned to celebrate the December 25 birthday of the major Roman god Mithras. And when the magi rose each morning, they couldn't put on a fresh cotton shirt. Or lessen the boredom of the long days by pulling out a Walkman and listening to a tape of Handel's *Messiah*. Or turn on a laptop and get a thumbnail history of Judaism from *Encarta*. T. S. Eliot rightly reflects the magi's perspective in "Journey of the Magi": "A hard time we had of it."[2]

Traditionally, the visit of the magi is viewed as a significant sign that the babe offers hope for all people who seek full and authentic life. We know little about those visitors. The term *magi* originally referred to the Persian learned priestly caste and later referred to those skilled in occult power and knowledge.[3] As learned men, they may have heard of the major world religions of their day—central Asia's Hinduism, India's Buddhism, China's Confucianism and Taoism, and Japan's Shintoism. They probably knew that Roman culture had a crowded gallery of gods and goddesses in addition to Mithras (who was worshiped as the invincible god who gave life and maintained justice and truth[4]). They obviously had heard of Judaism but were unaware of the prophecy that the Messiah was to be born in Bethlehem like King David.

What we do know about the magi is that they were awake enough to their surroundings to see the star. And they had the courage to follow it, which meant a long journey from the East (perhaps from Mesopotamia, the home of astrology in the Hellenistic period[5]). They even had the courage to disobey Herod for the sake of the child. Upon reaching Jerusalem, they began asking around town about the child "born king of the Jews" whose star they'd seen. That piqued Herod's royal paranoia. Calling for them secretly, he requested their return after they found the child because (lying with a grin) he wanted also to "go and pay him homage" (Matt. 2:7-8).

When the magi set out after leaving the king, the star went ahead of them and stopped over the place of the child, which now, according to Matthew, is a house. These men were Gentiles not Jews, foreigners not natives, and traditionally represent a different heritage, worldview, and race—and they "were overwhelmed with joy." They entered and "saw the child with Mary his mother; and they knelt down and paid him homage. Then, opening their treasure chests, they offered him gifts of gold, frankincense, and myrrh" (Matt. 2:10-11). According to Kelsey, the first gift came from Persia's mines, the second from Arabia's balsam trees, and the third from rare trees in the East.[6] The last we know of the magi from Matthew is that they leave for their country by another road.

✥

If we do glimpse the star during our Advent adventure and dare to follow it, we may find ourselves unwilling or unable to give our gifts. The magi's gifts remind us that each person has a special gift to offer. For various reasons, many of us hold back the gift with which God endowed us. Sometimes that gift cries to us from the distant past. We recall the dream that existed before the tollway. We remember the passion that called out for expression before practicality snuffed out a precious piece of our life, the vocation we knew we were meant to fulfill, that yearning from yesteryear. It falls upon us now like the still chill of the catacombs.

Like the magi, we have a hard time of it.

This babe whom the magi honored is the One who still offers us new hope in our search for full and authentic life. He is the One who comforts us with awareness that it is not too late to set out on the journey. It is not too late to integrate our dream with duty, our passion with practicality, our youthful yearning with mature wisdom. It is not too late to recover that special gift we were given to share with others.

I believe that God gave me the gift of writing. I have sensed this from childhood but only in the last decade could I responsibly commit to this call. Writing is an arduous process for me, and I face it with a vulnerable heart. I stare at a blank page of paper, hoping to fill it with words neither vague nor vain; turning toward the loving Holy One, seeking to be a source of blessing through the writing; stretching beyond myself through words both kept and tossed and lifting the pen, however feeble the result, with gratitude and reverence. Always with reverence.

The Comforter tells us to set out! It is not too late! It will never be too late!

Referring to the magi as "seekers," Kelsey says,

> They knew the dangers of deserts and mountain passes, as well as of the bandits who preyed on travelers. They knew all this before starting, and yet their vision was worth the gamble. The Magi were spiritual adventurers.[7]

We are invited to join them on the journey, to be seekers, spiritual adventurers.

When we try to live with God and walk with Jesus Christ, each day offers a spiritual adventure; and we decide anew every day, as did the magi, whether the vision is worth the risk. This spiritual adventure calls for flexibility and openness to surprise. And patience. And trust, especially trust. At the end of each day's adventure, we silently kneel before the babe. Overwhelmed with joy we pay him homage; we open our treasure chest and offer him our gift. Unlike the magi, we don't have to return home—for there on our knees offering our gift, we *are* home.

Giving and Thanksgiving
Scripture: John 1:1-14

All during our Advent adventure, the sun has been later to rise each day and sooner to set. We have stumbled through the long, dark nights, yearning for the light. Now the time of the winter solstice is here, the beginning of longer days, the ending of shorter nights. "The light shines in the darkness, and the darkness did not overcome it" (John 1:5). Giving and thanksgiving are our dance of grateful response.

On Christmas morning we will give presents to the people we love. Christmas exists to celebrate the birth of the Christ, and the deeper purpose of giving a Christmas present is to remember Jesus' birth with gratitude and, like the magi, to honor him. As we give a present to someone close, can we imagine saying, "This is for you in honor and grateful remembrance of the Christ child"? If not aloud, suppose we whisper those words silently within our own souls. That kind of giving and thanksgiving would change our focus and perhaps even our choice of gifts.

The season of giving and thanksgiving is year-round and lifelong, and all of us have "gift" stories to tell. One of the highlights of my life came when my daughter-in-law Angela gave me the gift of inviting me to help after the birth of their third child, Graham. What a joy it was to be with that beloved family and feel useful. What a privilege to clean and do laundry, cook and iron for them (though the stove and iron will be the last appliances worn out in my own home). What a delight to hold that darling baby. To do the things that allowed his mother some leisure time, to play with Chelsea and Sarah, to catch the happy smile on my son's face. Now Graham is two, and every time I look at his impish little smile, I think of those joyful days. What a gift Angela gave me!

Another family gift that stands out to me occurred when my daughter Valerie was attending Chicago University School of Divinity. The two of us were hurrying to catch the view of the sunset from the World Trade Center when I slipped on my slick, wet shoe soles in the middle of State Street and broke my wrist. Valerie blessed me with complete role reversal. She knew which hospital to go to and where it was. She sat with me attentively, being a loving presence and ready to be my advocate if needed. She took care of me in such a way that even in a Chicago emergency room that brought television's *ER* to real life, I felt secure, for I was in her good hands. What a gift Valerie gave me!

My father gave me a gift when I was nine years old, one that still lives in me. He taught me how to fly a Cessna 140. He taught me how to take off and how to land, how to dive and spin and stall (the latter under great duress). Flying together brought us close, and it stands out more than any other childhood experience with him. That gift was more than simply flying a plane at nine. Somehow, for me, it came to symbolize an ongoing gift that has influenced me in times of need. When I felt fragmented by work, and the surrounding pressures moved in upon me like choking hands, I knew I could lift off to another level. When I found myself in a tight situation, I knew I could land on a short runway. When my life seemed to be in a dive or a spin, I knew I could pull out again. And I knew that even a stall was not permanent. I still know all that, and it serves me well. What a gift my father gave me!

I could unwrap other treasured gifts from every person in my family. But three is a good symbolic number, in keeping with the magi. All of us have stories of giving and thanksgiving, important stories to remember and to share. All of us also know stories about being in the darkness and not being overcome. These stories too are about giving and thanksgiving.

"The light shines in the darkness, and the darkness did not overcome it." I recall a British writer I heard speak recently. Her talk reflected her Christianity, and during the question-and-answer period that followed, a person in the audience asked how she had become a Christian. "I didn't grow up in a church home," came the honest answer. "I was ambitious, had achieved everything I wanted by a young age—and managed to lose it all. Then I began to wonder about God. So I went to the library and looked under *G* for God. And I haven't stopped reading and learning since." We see the star shining not in daylight but in darkness.

"The light shines in the darkness, and the darkness did not overcome it." Once I saw an elderly, blind woman who would not let darkness overcome her. The sun came out, warming the winter day after a prolonged cold spell, and people of all ages came to the park to lift their faces toward the sky and snuggle up to the sunbeams. Pines scented the air, their tiny cones dotting the snow; and children at play laughed in the background.

The woman moved her cane side-to-side in front of her and slowly followed the snow-shoveled path to the green park bench. She sat down, hooked her cane over the wooden armrest, and began folding her woolen scarf, her nimble fingers feeling the edges and corners. She put the neat square in her shopping bag and removed her worn Bible, laying it open on her lap. With unconcealed devotion, she placed her hands on the open Bible, palms down, and lifted her head upward. Her lips were smiling, her face radiant, and a sense of peace filled the space around her. She sat silently, as though her wrinkled hands were absorbing the words her old eyes could not see.

After a long while the woman bowed her head, and her unfocused eyes seemed to stare at the Bible, her mind seeing words and images no longer visible in her blindness. She began to move her index fingers slowly across the two pages, her left on the left-hand page, her right on the right-hand one, as though she were reading the lines simultaneously. Her hands danced with graceful reverence back and forth across the pages.

The woman's eyes could not read the words, but her heart knew them. She saw nothing; she saw everything. She walked in darkness; she danced in light. She too, as W. H. Auden spoke about the magi, was "led by the light of an unusual star."[8]

As we look at that tranquil woman, we yearn for a special place to draw away for a while and find our own centered space where we can see the light and practice the spiritual disciplines (for example, prayer, fasting, silence, scripture reading, solitude, simplicity, study, service). Perhaps we prefer to be in a secluded place alone outdoors or to gaze through the east window at sunrise or to light a candle on a small table set aside as an altar. We long for the inner power to go into that centered space without going to that special place—like the woman on the park bench amidst children at play.

We can all tell stories of reclaiming the star, of how the darkness did not overcome the light, stories of giving and thanksgiving. I remember a summer day filled with light when my daughter Danna Lee was in college, and we rode horses to the top of Bristol Head, a 12,000-foot mountain in the Rockies. On its flat crest was a meadow made beautiful with hundreds of Old-Man-of-the-Mountain wildflowers. Their petals were golden yellow, and their dark button eyes all looked toward the sun, turning gradually from east to west as dawn met dusk. Those little flowers bloomed their story of giving and thanksgiving, following the largest star of all across the sky. "The light shines in the darkness, and the darkness did not overcome it."

❖

One seasonal tradition is to light candles in an Advent wreath, one for each of the four Sundays of Advent plus the Christ candle in the center, which we light on Christmas Eve or Christmas Day. Families who carry out this tradition at home find the memory of many stories woven over the years among the greenery of the wreath. Like dripped wax on a candle, the past lingers in the present. And the vision we hold today rises like smoke, drifting into the future. In reclaiming the star, we glance backward and look forward, glance inward and look outward, dancing to the rhythm of memory and vision, of soul time and service time. In the poem "East Coker," T. S. Eliot proclaims,

"So the darkness shall be the light, and the stillness the dancing."[9]

We dance toward the star and the stable, ever closer to the Stillness and the Light that reshape and transform us.

THOUGHTS AND REFLECTIONS

✦ When did you most feel the presence of God this week? When did you least feel the presence of God this week?

✦ Reflect on your own journey to Bethlehem. What parts of your experience resemble Mary's journey? What "bread" does the journey offer? What bedlam?

✦ What special gift has God given you? How are you able to fulfill that gift, that vocation, in your occupation or your leisure time?

✦ Reflect on a time when you walked in darkness, and the darkness did not overcome you. If you feel comfortable, share the story.

✦ Share a story about giving and thanksgiving.

✦ Consider how you give Christmas gifts. In what way does your giving remember and honor the Christ child? What might you do so your giving could become a remembrance and honoring of the Christ child? Share your insights.

Note to Adventurers reading this book daily: Because Advent begins the fourth Sunday before Christmas, the last week varies in length. The first Sunday can be as early as November 27, which means the fourth week will have six days (December 18–23). Or the first Sunday of Advent can be as late as December 3, which means Christmas Eve falls on that fourth Sunday, leaving no days in the fourth week. Because of this variance, adjust your fourth-week reading appropriately. If this week of Advent has more than three days, reflect on the following scriptures, one each day as needed: Psalm 24; Psalm 89:1-4; Micah 5:2-5. Write your own meditative prayer.

Recalling the Story, Restoring the Call

HE STABLE STORY is two millennia old; and throughout these centuries, threads of myth, legend, and
folklore have been interwoven—Santa Claus, elves,
and Rudolph to name only three. These stories
sometimes merge with (or submerge) the story of Mary and Joseph
and the babe in the manger. We bring our Advent adventure to a close
by recalling the story, the simple and sacred story with nothing added
and nothing taken away. And in response, we restore our call—whether
as clergy in ministry primarily within the church or as laity in ministry
primarily in the world. In *The Good Negress* by A. J. Verdelle, Neesey's
grandmother consoles her:

> "Neesey, I know you upset. I know how lonesome you
> feelin,…But you let Granmama tell you somethin. The best way to
> make y'self feel better is to get y'hands to workin. When you put
> y'hands on somethin and make it somethin else, that will heal you
> lower places than you cry from."[1]

We restore our call by putting our hands and heads and
hearts to work in ministry to God's world.

A friend told me about her grandchild who had just received a crisp, new twenty-dollar bill for her birthday—a great deal of money to her. She had it with her in church on Christmas Eve. The joyous service included a living Nativity, choir, bells, candles, and, of course, the Christmas story. The pastor announced that the special offering would provide meals for the homeless and feed the hungry children of the city. She opened her small, red purse and took out the twenty-dollar bill.

Her grandmother saw her and, meaning well, whispered, "You don't have to give that."

The child smiled up at her grandmother. "I want to."

"I'll give you some change, so you won't have to give it all."

"I *want* to give it all." And with great joy she did, holding nothing back.

This little girl gives us a wonderful example of recalling the story and restoring the call.

A six-year-old boy at a groundbreaking for a new church offers us another example. The children received small, yellow, plastic "hard" hats for the event, and we all stood together in the field. Since it was fall, beautiful wildflowers of different kinds, all of them yellow, covered the ground. During the service this little boy wandered over to the side of the crowd, took off his hard hat, and began picking the flowers and putting them in it. Then he brought them back for his mother.

This child illustrates our Advent adventure, which has invited us to form new habits (a process that supposedly takes only three weeks). He shows us how to begin opening our eyes to the beautiful meadow of gifts that God provides, instead of trudging along with downcast eyes, watching for landmines. And he shows us how to risk removing our hard hat of self-protection and defensiveness, turning it into a basket to receive God's manifold gifts, and then giving them away to another.

We recall the story and restore the call. Not someday but today. Each day. Holding nothing back. A line from "The Chambered Nautilus" by Oliver Wendell Holmes echoes the call of Advent: "Leave thy low-vaulted past!"[2]

The Manger
Scripture: Psalm 98

For many years now I have taken for granted the magical celebration of Christmas Eve and Christmas Day with family gathered and traditional trappings and making good memories—until last Christmas. On the day before Christmas Eve, a severe winter storm stranded Bill and me midjourney. We were caught between our home in Dallas and our daughter's home in Colorado Springs where the family was gathering for Christmas. We faced our first celebration of these holy days totally separated from other loved ones.

It was a Christmas stripped of tree, stockings, and family rituals that have evolved over the years. Since Bill and I had exchanged our gifts before leaving home, it was also the first Christmas in our lives without the privilege of giving a single gift. Our gifts for the family shouted at us from their heap in the corner of the room.

Because of its place in our family traditions, I'd brought along the old crèche from Jerusalem. Once more—as on the first Sunday of Advent—I unwrapped each of the figures. But this time they sat on a lamp table beside the pile of wrapped gifts. Again the figures took me back to the essentials of the story: the simplicity of the stable sheltering Mary and Joseph, the manger smelling of hay where Jesus lay, the animals staring at the infant lying in their feed trough, the shepherds in awe, the magi with their gifts, and the light of the star. Those figures relate the essence of the story.

On Christmas Eve, Bill and I attended a beautiful, old church, ending Advent as it had begun—with strangers in an unfamiliar community of faith. Yet once again, these strangers were our kin. Our son Bryant had reminded me by phone that everyone in the family, wherever we were, would be in church that night. "All of us will probably sing 'Silent Night,'" he said, "and we can think of each other as we sing it." His words became a comforting gift.

Sure enough! Bill and I held hands with our pew neighbors as the congregation sang that beautiful Austrian carol written on Christmas Eve in 1818. Even though our grown children and our small grandchildren were miles and miles away, I felt linked to them, for they too were singing "Silent Night" (perhaps also teary-eyed), hearing the reading of Luke, praying, taking Communion. In a most powerful way, I felt their presence in this absence and bowed my heart in awe and gratitude.

Neither Bill nor I had ever before experienced these holy days without props, presents, or people we know. In that experience, however, was the gift of blessing. Nothing distracted us from the power of Love in the manger. It was a Christmas not lost in the trappings but wrapped in the Christ, a Christmas, a *Christ*-mass.

And that is enough. That is the purpose. All else is superimposed. The rest adds, of course, to the wonder and joy of these holy days and to the making of good memories. But nothing else—*nothing else*—is part of the essential story except the babe in the manger who brings hope and faith and love to our lives, giving us meaning and purpose and showering us with grace.

The Mystery
Scripture: Luke 2:7-20

Two thousand years ago God spoke through a manger, and we still experience the mystery! The Christmas story is filled with it. Mystery is not in what we see and do not understand. Mystery is in what we know deeply and cannot see.

I recall a crisp, silent night during Christmastide when my children were teenagers, and we cross-country skied in the moonlight. The sky switched on its tiny lights above us, and the moonglow lit the way. Spruce limbs drooped with icy fingers and cast crooked shadows all around us. The swoosh-swoosh of our skis startled the silence. A stream trickled beneath the ice, heeding the call of the sea. The soil hid beneath the snow, and seeds slept deep below, trusting the green of spring. Leafless aspen gazed at us from the other side of the pond, singing softly with the spruce in antiphonal chorus "Il Est Né": "He is born, the holy Child." We stopped, glancing back at the twin scars trailing behind us marking clearly where we'd been. But where we would go lay open before us, unmarred. We grew quiet, sensing anew that the stillness of the universe is a dance of barefoot grace with the Creator, a silence alive with cosmic joy and mystery.

Emmanuel! God is with us!

O sing to the Lord a new song,
  for he has done marvelous things (Ps. 98:1).
We hold a new babe in the palms of our hands
  and see God in the mystery and wonder of birth.
We reach out our arms to receive a child's hug
  and see God in the mystery of our love returned.
We smile at a teen who comes bouncing along
  and see God in the mystery of youth's dreams unfurled.
We touch a lined face mapping lost youthful dreams
  and see God in the mystery of new beauty and grace.

Let the floods clap their hands;
  let the hills sing together for joy (Ps. 98:8).
We watch the sun rise on a snow-covered peak
  and see God in the mystery of hope each new day.
We stand in the sand on a beautiful shore
  and see God in the mystery of the rolling surf.
We climb craggy rocks where a columbine grows
  and see God in the mystery of the strength to bloom.
We view a blue butterfly soaring uphill
  and see God in the mystery of still-life flight.
We stare at the sky on the darkest of nights
  and see God in the mystery of the stars above.

Make a joyful noise to the Lord, all the earth:
  break forth into joyous song and sing praises.
Sing praises to the Lord with the lyre,
  with the lyre and the sound of melody (Ps. 98:4–5).
We hear the *Messiah* and well up with joy
  and see God in the mystery of the human soul.
We bow at the manger with reverence and awe
  and know God in the mystery of the babe we call Christ.

Emmanuel! God is with us!

Guides for Adventurers

GUIDE FOR INDIVIDUALS

THE INTRODUCTION SUGGESTS a format for reading this book. You may choose to follow your soul in your own reflection on the scriptures and the book or use the following outline as a "guided" adventure:

Recentering through silence and prayer

There are many ways to pray, none of them wrong. A daily prayer as you walk through our Advent adventure—a silent, ongoing prayer that becomes as much a part of you as breathing—can help keep you mindful of holiness, wholeness. Today I offer this one with the suggestion that you write your own unique prayer:

> O Lord, help me to have a sense of your presence at all times and in all things today. May what I do today be done facing toward you. May I do nothing today that leads me away from you—not through my deeds, words, nor even my thoughts. Today, may the sacred be rekindled in my life. Amen.

A time of wordless silence is also an important part of prayer.

Reading and reflecting on the scriptures

Just as there are many ways to pray, so too there are many ways to read the scriptures. Consider reflecting on what a scripture passage means to you in your own life today. What does this passage say to you? Where does it apply to your life? How can you respond?

Reading *Manger and Mystery*

Read one chapter a week during the four weeks of Advent. Read chapter 5 in preparation for Christmas Eve and Christmas Day.

Reflecting on "Thoughts and Reflections"

Receiving and celebrating God's grace

Remember that God loves you unconditionally.

Rejoicing in God's gifts

Recall God's many gifts to you in the past, the gifts through loved ones who surround you now and the gifts of nature. Express your gratitude to God and, as occasions arise, to the people who bless your life.

Returning to God's world with a prayerful heart

GUIDE FOR GROUPS

OUR ADVENT ADVENTURE can be a bold undertaking in which we expose ourselves to uncertainty about our personal and communal destination, welcome surprises along the way, and trust the Holy Spirit. As Adventurers in community, we covenant together—not to the group or to the book—but to our journey of faith in Jesus Christ. We make this covenant with one another. In this covenant we support one another in the adventure, and we hold one another accountable. We express this covenant by

- praying and reading the scriptures daily;
- attending each session and seeing this as sacred time in communion with God and our fellow Advent Adventurers;
- reading the designated chapter of *Manger and Mystery* (I recommend reading portions daily if you practice a time of solitude);
- being open to the breath of the Spirit and expecting to grow as persons and as a group.

As Adventurers we will honor these community courtesies:

- To listen in love, without disapproval of other Adventurers and to share in truth (as we perceive it);
- To value individual uniqueness and to welcome fresh perspectives, recognizing that the richness of diversity helps us grow;
- To face differences openly, treating one another with respect and applying the RSV translation of Isaiah 1:18: "Come now, let us reason together" rather than that of the NRSV: "Come now, let us argue it out"!
- To honor requests for confidentiality.

A WORD FOR LEADERS

Before the group meets, you as leader will need to see that Adventurers have their books and know to read the first chapter in advance of the first meeting. Notice the special preparation for the final session. As a leader within the group, your primary task is not to teach but to journey with the other Adventurers and to facilitate the adventure. The leader has six major responsibilities:

1. To begin and end each session on time.

2. To be sure everyone understands the format for reading the book, and to make clear the reading assignment each week.

3. To follow the guide when appropriate for the group but not to see it as an "assignment" to be accomplished. Trust where the Spirit leads the Adventurers.

4. To facilitate group sharing so no one dominates, and everyone has equal opportunities to share without feeling pressured to do so. (A group of ten people would mean that each person's fair share—including the leader's—is ten percent of the time allotted.)

5. To set the tone for the sessions as a warm, comfortable, and stimulating place to be. A centering symbol might help; for example, lighting the appropriate candle(s) in an Advent wreath before beginning the "Recentering" time.

6. To close each session on a hopeful, accepting, caring note.

Since each person is a unique creation of God, we celebrate our differences rather than fear them. Though our silence together may feel a bit uneasy in the beginning, we will become more comfortable with it as the adventure continues.

1   RECOVERING THE STABLE

(First Week in Advent)

Recentering through prayer for guidance and a time of silence

Reading the scripture: 1 Corinthians 1:3-9

Be attentive to the reading of the scripture as though you are a Christian before the invention of the printing press (mid-fifteenth century) and will never have your own Bible. Your only access to the scriptures is by hearing them read aloud. Listen from that perspective. After the reading, consider what that experience was like for you.

Reflecting and sharing

Allow the "Thoughts and Reflections" section at the end of the chapter to guide your discussion.

Receiving and celebrating God's grace

Go around the circle, receiving and giving a word of grace. Words or gestures of acceptance, forgiveness, assurance, and thanksgiving are appropriate ways to receive and celebrate grace.

Rejoicing in God's gifts

Share something for which you were grateful this week.

Renewing the covenant

✥ Go around the circle and share something that you feel led to a change in the way you prepare for the birth of the Christ child.

✥ Go around the circle again and pray (*by name*) for the person to your right, praying for his or her desired change (*naming that change*).

✥ Continue the Advent adventure of praying, reading and reflecting on scripture, and reading *Manger and Mystery* during the week. (Read chapter 2 for next week.)

✥ Pray daily for the Adventurer on your right (*by name*), including his or her desired change.

✦ Try journaling as part of your adventure by recording Advent thoughts, images, and signposts. (This might take the form of a page a day, a poem, a song, a sketch or a painting.)

Returning to God's world

Close with prayer, sending the Adventurers forth with prayerful hearts into God's world.

2   REKINDLING THE SACRED

(Second Week in Advent)

Recentering through prayer for guidance and a time of silence

Reading the scripture: Psalm 96

One way to read the scriptures is to place yourself in them—becoming a participant instead of an observer. As the scripture is read, open your imagination and senses (seeing, hearing, smelling, touching, tasting) and be there. After the reading, consider these questions: What did you see? hear? smell? What textures or temperatures did you feel? What could you taste?

Reflecting and sharing

Allow the "Thoughts and Reflections" section at the end of the chapter to guide your discussion.

Receiving and celebrating God's grace

Go to the person who prayed for you and to the person for whom you prayed, receiving and giving a word of grace.

Rejoicing in God's gifts

Share something for which you were grateful this week.

Renewing the covenant

⊕ Answer in your heart, reflecting silently after each question: Did you keep your covenant with this group this week to pray and read the scripture daily? Did you read chapter 2 of the book? Did you pray daily for the Adventurer you were assigned last week? Did you move toward making the change you desired?

⊕ Go around the circle and share something that you feel led to change in order to rekindle the sacred in your life.

⊕ Go around the circle again and pray (*by name*) for the person to your left, praying for his or her desired change (*naming that change*).

⊕ Continue the Advent adventure of praying, reading and reflecting on the scriptures, and reading *Manger and Mystery* (chapter 3 for next week).

✦ Pray daily for the Adventurer on your left (*by name*), including his or her desired change.

✦ Continue journaling if meaningful to you.

Returning to God's world

Close with prayer, sending the Adventurers forth with prayerful hearts into God's world.

3 REMEMBERING THE SONG

(Third Week in Advent)

Recentering through prayer for guidance and a time of silence

Reading the scripture: 1 Thessalonians 5:16-24

Bonhoeffer said that the scripture has something to say not only to the church but also to us personally today for our own Christian life. Listen to the scripture in that light and then consider its personal meaning for you.

Reflecting and sharing

Allow the "Thoughts and Reflections" section at the end of the chapter to guide your discussion.

Receiving and celebrating God's grace

Go to the person who prayed for you and to the person for whom you prayed, receiving and giving a word of grace.

Rejoicing in God's gifts

✤ Share something for which you were grateful this week.

✤ Create a "song" of praise as a group by going around the circle beginning with the leader, and each person adding a sentence "verse" that rejoices in God.

Renewing the covenant

✤ Answer in your heart, reflecting silently after each question: Did you keep your covenant with this group this week to pray and read the scripture daily? Did you read chapter 3 of the book? Did you pray daily for the Adventurer assigned to you last week? Did you take a step toward your desired change?

✤ Go around the circle and share something that has been meaningful to you on this adventure.

✤ Continue the Advent adventure of praying, reading and reflecting on the scripture, and reading *Manger and Mystery* (chapter 4 for next week).

✦ Pray daily for the Adventurer sitting across from you (*by name*).

✦ Continue journaling if meaningful to you.

Returning to God's world

Close with prayer, sending the Adventurers forth with prayerful hearts into God's world. Ask everyone to bring an item next week that symbolizes the "gift" God has given them.

Note to leader: Next week's session provides a closing that you may use or adapt for use by the group. Allow the last twenty to thirty minutes (depending upon the size of your group) for this closing. You will need a candle in a candle holder for each member; the following figures from a crèche: Mary, Joseph, the baby, two (or more) shepherds, the wise men; and people assigned to read the scriptures. If your group would feel uncomfortable singing "Silent Night" together, arrange for one of them to sing a solo or take a recording and a player. You also may want to bring a cloth to cover all or part of the table on which group members will place the crèche figures, the symbolic gifts, and the candles.

4 RECLAIMING THE STAR

(Fourth Week in Advent)

Recentering through prayer for guidance and a time of silence

Reflecting and sharing

Allow the "Thoughts and Reflections" section at the end of the chapter to guide your discussion. (Remember to stop the discussion in time for the closing.)

Closing

(Place a cloth on the table, and have a candle in its holder for each Adventurer.)

Leader

"Let us share in the reading of the scriptures."

Adventurer 1 reads Luke 1:26-38.
Place the figure of Mary in the center of the table.

Adventurer 2 reads Matthew 1:18-25.
Place the figure of Joseph in the center of the table.

Adventurer 3 reads Luke 1:39-45.

Adventurer 4 reads Luke 1:46-55.

Adventurer 5 reads Luke 1:67-79.

Adventurer 6 reads Luke 2:1-7.
Place the baby Jesus in the center of the table.

Adventurer 7 reads Luke 2:8-20.
Place the shepherds in the center of the table.

Adventurer 8 reads Matthew 2:1-12.
Place the wise men in the center of the table.

Leader

"All of us have been given special gifts by God. I place this [*name item*] on the table as a symbol of my gift of [*name gift*]. (*Place the item near the crèche.*)

The leader may then instruct the Adventurers as follows:

"As you feel led, place your symbol on the table, name it, and state the name of the gift it symbolizes. You may prefer simply to place your item on the table. If you did not bring an item to share, feel free to say aloud what you intended to bring and its symbolism." [*Allow time for all Adventurers to share their gifts.*]

Leader

Offer a prayer of appreciation for the gifts of the group members. Then light your candle (from the Advent wreath if used) and say a word of blessing and appreciation to the person on your right and light his or her candle.

Adventurers

Continue the same process around the room.

All

Place candles on the table amidst the symbolic gifts. Then turn out the lights and sing (or listen to) "Silent Night."

Leader

"We are sent forth to reflect the light of God's love and laughter; to celebrate the mystery of the manger—year-round and lifelong; and, to follow Mother Teresa's suggestion of spending time each day in adoration of our Lord and doing nothing we know is wrong. Amen."

Notes

ONE: RECOVERING THE STABLE

1. Morton Kelsey, *The Drama of Christmas: Letting Christ into Our Lives* (Louisville, Ky.: Westminster John Knox, 1994), 4.
2. John Wesley, *The Works of John Wesley*, 3rd ed. (Peabody, Mass.: Henrickson Publishers, 1991), 12:254.
3. David Whyte, *The Heart Aroused: Poetry and the Preservation of the Soul in Corporate America* (New York: Doubleday, 1994), 220–21.
4. Jan Karon, *Out to Canaan* (New York: Penguin, 1997), 330.
5. James C. Fenhagen, *Invitation to Holiness* (Harrisburg, Pa.: Morehouse, 1991), 55.
6. Owen Chadwick, ed., *Western Asceticism* (Philadelphia, Pa.: Westminster, 1958), 100.
7. Whyte, 271.
8. David Steindl-Rast, *Gratefulness, the Heart of Prayer: An Approach to Life in Fullness* (New York: Paulist, 1984), 193.
9. W. H. Auden, "Precious Five," *Collected Poems* (New York: Vintage Books, 1991), 591.
10. Dietrich Bonhoeffer, *Life Together* (New York: Harper & Brothers, 1954), 82.
11. Pierre Teilhard de Chardin, *The Divine Milieu* (New York: Harper and Row, 1960), 66.
12. Steindl-Rast, 116.
13. *Ibid.*

14. C. S. Lewis, *Letters to Malcolm: Chiefly on Prayer* (London: Fontana, 1966), 77.

15. Joan D. Chittister, *The Rule of Benedict: Insights for the Ages* (New York: Crossroad, 1997), 23–24.

16. Steindl-Rast, v.

17. Charles Frazier, *Cold Mountain* (New York: Atlantic Monthly Press, 1997), 75.

18. Chittister, 27.

19. Cited in Charles Cole, "Spiritual Migrations," *New World Outlook*, New Series 58, no. 4 (March/April 1998): 27.

20. Andrew M. Greeley, *Lord of the Dance* (New York: Warner Books, 1984), 311.

21. Henri J. M. Nouwen, *Bread for the Journey: A Daybook of Wisdom and Faith* (San Francisco: HarperSanFrancisco, 1997), May 10.

22. *Ibid.*

23. Karon, 333–34.

24. Frazier, 121.

TWO: REKINDLING THE SACRED

1. Howard Thurman, *The Inward Journey* (Richmond, Ind.: Friends United Press, 1971), 44.

2. Cited in Whyte, 211.

3. P. D. James, *A Certain Justice* (New York: Alfred A. Knopf, 1997), 42–43.

4. T. S. Eliot, "The Dry Salvages," *Four Quartets* (London: Faber and Faber, 1959), 50.

5. Quoted in Robert Faricy, *The Spirituality of Teilhard de Chardin* (Minneapolis, Minn.: Winston, 1981), 84.

6. Steindl-Rast, 201.

7. Chittister, 30–31.

8. Macrina Wiederkehr, *A Tree Full of Angels: Seeing the Holy in the Ordinary* (San Francisco: Harper & Row, 1988), 26.

9. Whyte, 263.

10. Sally Eauclaire, "Allan Houser Carves His Own Destiny," *New Mexico Magazine*, August 1991: 68–69.

11. Frazier, 216.

12. Nouwen, May 6, May 5, May 7.

13. Margaret J. Wheatley and Myron Kellner-Rogers, *A Simpler Way* (San Francisco: Berrett-Koehler, 1996), 93.
14. Wheatley and Kellner-Rogers, 94.
15. Steindl-Rast, 96.
16. Quoted in Thomas Keating, *Invitation to Love: The Way of Christian Contemplation* (New York: Continuum, 1996), 38.
17. Frank McCourt, *Angela's Ashes: A Memoir* (New York: Scribner, 1996), 72.
18. Nouwen, April 4.
19. Wesley, 7:430.
20. Wendell Berry, *Fidelity: Five Stories* (New York: Pantheon Books, 1992), 50.
21. Steindl-Rast, 183.
22. Mary Bosanquet, *The Life and Death of Dietrich Bonhoeffer* (New York: Harper & Row, 1968), 70.
23. Georgia O'Keeffe, *Georgia O'Keeffe* (New York: Viking, 1976), unpaginated.
24. O'Keeffe, unpaginated.
25. Lewis, 93.
26. Chittister, 24.
27. Chittister, 38.
28. Steindl-Rast, 37.
29. Whyte, 176.

THREE: REMEMBERING THE SONG

1. Nouwen, February 18.
2. Chadwick, 156.
3. Chadwick, 169.
4. *Ibid.*
5. Chadwick, 184.
6. Chadwick, 99.
7. Chadwick, 97.
8. McCourt, 156.
9. Chadwick, 97.
10. Such as King James Version, New King James, Revised Standard, New Revised Standard, American Standard, New American, New Jerusalem, or New International.

11. Nouwen, April 6.
12. Pat Conroy, *Beach Music* (New York: Bantam Books, 1996), 773.
13. Walter Isaacson, "Our Century...And the Next One," *Time* 151, no. 14 (April 13, 1998): 34, 35.
14. Kelsey, 88.
15. Chadwick, 165.
16. Nouwen, April 9.
17. Chadwick, 185.
18. Conroy, 525.
19. McCourt, 97.
20. Wesley, 3:307.
21. Rueben P. Job, *A Wesleyan Spiritual Reader* (Nashville, Tenn.: Abingdon, 1997), 31.
22. Wesley, 6:126–28, 130–31.
23. Wesley, 6:131.
24. Wesley, 6:133.

FOUR: RECLAIMING THE STAR

1. Job, *A Wesleyan Spiritual Reader*, 76.
2. T. S. Eliot, "Journey of the Magi," *The Complete Poems and Plays 1909–1950* (New York: Harcourt Brace Jovanovich, 1971), 68.
3. "The Gospel According to Matthew" in *The Jerome Biblical Commentary,* eds. Raymond E. Brown, Joseph A. Fitzmyer, and Roland E. Murphy (Englewood Cliffs, N.J.: Prentice-Hall, 1968), 67.
4. Harold H. Rowley, ed., *New Atlas of the Bible* (New York: Doubleday, 1969), 139.
5. *The Jerome Biblical Commentary*, 67.
6. Kelsey, 61.
7. *Ibid.*
8. W. H. Auden, "For the Time Being" from *A Christmas Oratorio* in *The Collected Poetry of W. H. Auden* (New York: Random House, 1945), 442.
9. T. S. Eliot, "East Coker," *Four Quartets*, 28.

FIVE: RECALLING THE STORY, RESTORING THE CALL

1. A. J. Verdelle, *The Good Negress* (Chapel Hill, N.C.: Algonquin Books, 1995), 8.
2. Oliver Wendell Holmes, "The Chambered Nautilus," *Anthology of American Poetry*, ed. George Gesner (New York: Avenel Books, 1983), 192.

Selected Bibliography

Bonhoeffer, Dietrich. *Life Together*. New York: Harper & Brothers, 1954.

Chittister, Joan D. *The Rule of Benedict: Insights for the Ages*. New York: Crossroad, 1997.

Cole, Charles. "Spiritual Migrations." *New World Outlook*, New Series 58, no. 4 (March/April 1998): 27.

Eauclaire, Sally. "Allan Houser Carves His Own Destiny." *New Mexico Magazine* (August 1991): 58, 68–69.

Faricy, Robert. *The Spirituality of Teilhard de Chardin*. Minneapolis, Minn.: Winston, 1981.

Harper's Bible Commentary. Edited by James L. Mays. San Francisco: Harper & Row, 1988.

Harper's Bible Dictionary. Edited by Paul J. Achtemeier. San Francisco: HarperSanFrancisco, 1996.

Healey, Charles J. *Modern Spiritual Writers: Their Legacies of Prayer*. New York: Alba House, 1989.

The Interpreter's Bible. Edited by George Arthur Buttrick et al. Vol. 7, New York: Abingdon and Nashville, Tenn.: Cokesbury Press, 1951. Vol. 8, New York: Abingdon, 1952.

The Interpreter's Dictionary of the Bible. Edited by George Arthur Buttrick. New York: Abingdon, 1962.

Isaacson, Walter. "Our Century...And the Next One." *Time* 151, no. 14 (April 13, 1998): 30–37.

121

The Jerome Biblical Commentary. Edited by Raymond E. Brown, Joseph A. Fitzmyer, and Roland E. Murphy. Englewood Cliffs, N.J.: Prentice-Hall, 1968.

Job, Rueben P. *A Wesleyan Spiritual Reader*. Nashville, Tenn.: Abingdon, 1997.

Keating, Thomas. *Invitation to Love: The Way of Christian Contemplation*. New York: Continuum, 1996.

Kelsey, Morton. *The Drama of Christmas: Letting Christ into Our Lives*. Louisville, Ky.: Westminster John Knox, 1994.

Lehmann, Paul L. "The Foundation and Pattern of Christian Behavior." *Christian Faith and Social Action*. Edited by John A. Hutchison. New York: Charles Scribner's Sons, 1953.

The New Interpreter's Bible. Edited by Leander E. Keck et al. Vols. 8, 9. Nashville, Tenn.: Abingdon, 1995.

New Atlas of the Bible. Edited by Harold H. Rowley. New York: Doubleday, 1969.

Nouwen, Henri J. M. *Bread for the Journey: A Daybook of Wisdom and Faith*. San Francisco: HarperSanFrancisco, 1997.

Oden, William B. *Liturgy as Life-Journey*. Los Angeles: Acton House, 1976.

O'Keeffe, Georgia. *Georgia O'Keeffe*. New York: Viking, 1976.

Palmer, Parker J. *The Active Life: Wisdom for Work, Creativity, and Caring*. San Francisco: Harper Collins, 1991.

Steindl-Rast, David. *Gratefulness, the Heart of Prayer: An Approach to Life in Fullness*. New York: Paulist, 1984.

Weatherhead, Leslie D. *The Will of God*. Nashville, Tenn.: Abingdon, 1944.

Wesley, John. *The Works of John Wesley*. 3rd ed., Vols. 7, 12. Peabody, Mass.: Henrickson Publishers, 1991.

Western Asceticism. Edited by Owen Chadwick. Philadelphia, Pa.: Westminster, 1958.

The Westminster Dictionary of Christian Spirituality. Edited by Gordon S. Wakefield. Philadelphia, Pa.: Westminster, 1983.

The Westminster Dictionary of Worship. Edited by J. G. Davies. Philadelphia, Pa.: Westminster, 1972.

Wheatley, Margaret J. and Myron Kellner-Rogers. *A Simpler Way.* San Francisco: Berrett-Koehler, 1996.

Whyte, David. *The Heart Aroused: Poetry and the Preservation of the Soul in Corporate America.* New York: Doubleday, 1994.

About the Author

$\mathcal{M}$ARILYN BROWN ODEN is the author of seven books and coauthor of two additional ones. She leads spiritual renewal retreats for clergy and laity, has master's degrees both in counseling and creative writing, and is a member of First United Methodist Church in Dallas, Texas. She has been involved with children in various countries around the world. The smiles of the children above, from the Nyakatsapa Methodist School in Zimbabwe, capture Advent joy.